Universal Church *in Motion*

Synodal Paths

Edited by
Frank Ronge

Paulist Press
New York / Mahwah, NJ

Cover image Alexey_Hulsov / Pixabay.com
Cover design by Joe Gallagher
Book design by Lynn Else

Originally published in Germany. *Herder Thema - Weltkirche im Aufbruch. Synodale Wege.* Edited by Dr. Frank Ronge © 2022 Verlag Herder GmbH, Freiburg im Breisgau.

Library of Congress Cataloging-in-Publication Data
Names: Ronge, Frank, 1968– editor.
Title: Universal Church in motion: synodal paths / Frank Ronge, editor.
Description: New York; Mahwah, NJ : Paulist Press, [2024] | Originally published: Freiburg: Verlag Herder GmbH, 2023. | Summary: "This collection of chapters offers interesting and instructive insights to broaden readers' understanding of the Church and its many paths"—Provided by publisher.
Identifiers: LCCN 2023043034 (print) | LCCN 2023043035 (ebook) | ISBN 9780809156870 (paperback) | ISBN 9780809188529 (e-book)
Subjects: LCSH: Church renewal—Catholic Church. | Church—Catholicity. | Councils and synods. | Church polity.
Classification: LCC BX1747.5 .U55 2024 (print) | LCC BX1747.5 (ebook) | DDC 262/.52—dc23/eng/20231204
LC record available at https://lccn.loc.gov/2023043034
LC ebook record available at https://lccn.loc.gov/2023043035

ISBN 978-0-8091-5687-0 (paperback)
ISBN 978-0-8091-8852-9 (e-book)

Published by Paulist Press
997 Macarthur Boulevard
Mahwah, New Jersey 07430
www.paulistpress.com

Printed and bound in the
United States of America

CONTENTS

CONTENTS

Contents

FOREWORD

IS THE SYNODAL PATH on which the Catholic Church in Germany has embarked a special German path? Are Catholics in Germany dissociating themselves from the Universal Church and instead focusing their deliberations on questions not raised anywhere else in the Catholic Church? A more in-depth look at the various regions of the Universal Church quickly paints a different picture. This is precisely the view that this booklet seeks to open up for its readers. It asks whether considerations, dynamics, and issues are comparable across the countries and regions of the world—and in many cases, finds an answer.

One thing that becomes clear: the believers' interest in a Church that creates opportunities to participate, both in the field of diaconal commitment and in proclamation of the gospel—and not least in questions of leadership and decision-making—is not just great but is also rapidly growing. Pope Francis took up this dynamic at the right time by inviting the Universal Church to a great and shared Synodal Path. As far as the topics of the Synodal Path in Germany are concerned, however, it is also evident that these are addressed—in different ways, perhaps, but no less clearly—in many different places throughout the Universal Church. It is far from the case that it is in Germany alone that questions are being asked about a more transparent and participatory approach to power; about a more developed, more communicable ethics of relationships and sexuality; a more future-oriented priestly existence; and roles of greater responsibility and visibility for women in the Church.

Yes, and as this book also shows, the Universal Church is colorful and diverse. Diversity may be a challenging notion, but more than anything else it is a sign of vitality and a source of inspiration. We hope that reading this booklet will offer interesting and instructive insights and thus help broaden the reader's own horizons.

All those inclined to think that the Church should evolve as little as possible can now realize: the Church is home to a great dynamism that is an indispensable part of its essence. But all those who think that nothing will change anyway because—even if there is a good-faith desire in Germany to see needed reforms—the Universal Church will not go along with them, they need to know this: we, as Catholics in Germany, are not alone in these concerns; the Universal Church is in transition. But this gives us courage and hope for genuine change in a Church that credibly proclaims the good news and is sincerely concerned for the people, the "hearers of the word."

Copresidents of the Synodal Path:

Dr. Irme Stetter-Karp, president of the
Central Committee of German Catholics

Bishop Dr. Georg Batzing, chairman of the
German Bishops' Conference

Part I
SYNODALITY

SEEKING COUNSEL AND FINDING CONSENSUS

Rafael Luciani

Pope Francis recognizes synodality as the keyword for the third millennium. This involves more than a matter of words: synodality is an attitude, a process in which all stakeholders are learners, as it were. What is needed is reform from the grassroots.

POPE FRANCIS CALLS UPON the entire Church to seek a new model that will overcome unequal relationships, superiority, and subordination, and to initiate a dialogue that creates new ecclesiastical paths and structures for the third millennium. At the commemoration marking the fiftieth anniversary of the Synod of Bishops, he called for a deeper understanding of the ecclesiology of the people of God, pointing out that the path of synodality "is what the Lord expects from the Church of the third millennium." His urging occurred in a context in which a renewal of ecclesiastical life is more urgent than ever before.

The pope's dream of a Church that renews itself through internal consultations and counsel from outside, in a common search for consensus, is rooted in a nearly forgotten medieval tradition in which canon law has codified the principle "What touches all must be decided by all."

Synodal practices are thus not new to the Roman Catholic Church. The influential Cyprian of Carthage was also aware of something akin to the golden rule of synodality: "Nothing without the advice of the presbytery and the consensus of the people" was his maxim.

Stemming from the first millennium in the history of the Church, these two principles for action offer an adequate interpretive framework for reflection on the opportunities and challenges that the contemporary practice of synodality involves. For the bishop of Carthage, the focus was on communion in the Church. He developed methods based on dialogue and common discernment that enabled everyone, not just the presbyters, to take part in deliberations and decisions. These are two examples of a *forma ecclesiae* in which the exercise of power is understood as a shared responsibility.

Pope Francis seems to be inspired by this approach when he envisions a synodal Church as a listening Church: "It is necessary to listen to God until we hear the cry of the People with Him, and we need to listen to the People until we breathe the will to which God calls us."

Listening is indispensable in a synodal ecclesiology as it is rooted in recognition of the identity of ecclesial subjects and based on horizontal relationships that rest on the radicality of the dignity of all the baptized and on participation in the common priesthood of all the faithful (*Lumen Gentium* 10). The Church as a whole qualifies itself through processes of listening in which each ecclesial subject contributes something that completes the identity and mission of the other (*Apostolicam Actuositatem* 6), based on what is distinctive to each individual (29).

Such an understanding of the Church implies an overcoming of unequal relations of superiority and subordination and the transition to the logic of "mutual need" (*LG* 32). This is in keeping with the spirit of the International Theological Commission (ITC), which affirms that "[a] synodal Church is a Church of participation and co-responsibility" (Synodality in the Life and Mission of the Church). In its exercise of synodality, the Church is called upon to associate the participation of all, based on the calling of each individual, with the authority conferred by Christ on the College of Bishops and presided over by the pope.

Participation is based on the fact that all believers are able and called to place at the service of others their respective gifts received through the Holy Spirit. Every individual has a right to be heard, and it is the obligation of those who exercise authority to accept advice based on listening. One listens to a people, a place, and a time to perceive in these the voice of the Holy Spirit and to find ways that correspond to each epoch.

The Amazon Synod already made clear how identity building the listening process can be. This process can become even more dynamic in listening and in dialogue with the people, the realities and the history of their territory (cf. *Querida Amazonia* 66). Listening, however, is not an end in itself. In a process of listening, it is important to take all actions into account: praying, listening, analyzing, dialoguing, and advising. The destination of this path is not only to meet, listen, and get to know one another better but to work together so that pastoral decisions can be taken.

These are just a few aspects that define the meaning and aim of a synodal process. In the synod on synodality, the Church wants to make progress in the search "to give herself a more exhaustive definition"—as Paul VI observed at the reopening of the Second Vatican Council.

WHAT IS NEW ABOUT THE WORLD SYNOD?

The World Synodal Process is just the beginning of a long process that can lead to a deeper rapprochement among the various areas of Christian life: in the history, language, and culture that characterize interpersonal communication and its symbolic forms of expression. In their concrete lives, the people who participate promote the practice of a synodal style.

It is important to understand that synodality is the path best suited to developing ecclesial processes of identity formation and theological and cultural reorganization of the Church as a Church of Churches, presided over by the Bishop of the Church of Rome and in communion with all Churches.

If this is overlooked, one runs the risk of confining the grasp and practice of synodality to a purely affective and atmospheric practice, without effectively translating it into specific changes that would contribute toward transcending the current clerical institutional Church.

It was with this in mind that the Vatican employed a theological commission to advise throughout this process. This is a new development, one that restores cooperation between theology and the magisterium in a way that always should have existed.

A subcommission within this commission was set up to elaborate proposals for the reform of canon law. If what is heard is not implemented in the form of new ecclesiastical channels and structures, this will reveal another ecclesial model that does not adequately take the *sensus fidelium* into account.

All things considered, the current synod involves an important innovation: it is no longer an event but a process. It begins with an ecclesiology of the local churches. In the first, diocesan phase, the bishops must not only listen to the people of God, but also, as an integral part of this, join them in reflecting on pastoral decisions and elaborating these. According to the text of *Lumen Gentium* 12, which is invoked in *Episcopalis Communio* 5, it is the entirety of the faithful, "from Bishops to the last of the lay faithful, [who]... show universal agreement in matters of faith and morals."

It is not about the *sensus* of individual bishops, but about the *sensus* of the entire Church (*sensus ecclesiae totius populi*). This is why perhaps one of the most important challenges for the ecclesial hierarchy will be to create facilitators and procedures that will incorporate all the faithful while specifying the modalities of participation. The laity in particular are active subjects in the Church. Already in 2007, at the Aparecida Conference, the Latin American bishops put forth the idea of involving the laity in discernment, decision-making, planning, and execution (*Aparecida* 371).

If the approach of a synodal Church "not only has its point of departure but also its point of arrival in the People of God" (*Episcopalis Communio* 7), and if it is 'through synodality [that]...the Church reveals and configures herself as the pilgrim People of God' (ITC, Synodality, 42), then it is necessary to do everything possible to ensure that the age of the Church here and now leads to an authentic synodalization of the entire Church.

This will make it crucially important to identify and apply models of decision-making in the Church. One possible result could be to make decision-making binding on parish priests as they themselves have taken part in the process of listening and discerning, adopting counsel and building consensus, and thus agreeing to commit themselves.

Where decision-making is concerned, every model for the future of the Church must consider that its inherent synodal dimension must find expression through enacting and directing processes of participation and discernment.

These processes bear witness to the dynamism of communion that ultimately inspires all ecclesial decision-making (ITC, Synodality, 76). The major challenge will be to create a culture of ecclesial consensus that can manifest itself in the synodal styles, events, and structures from which a new ecclesial approach will emerge for the Church of the third millennium.

TWO AGES, TWO CHURCHES, ONE SPIRITUAL LIFE

Developments and changes of perspective promote community

Joan Chittister

Not letting the past determine the present, but learning from it instead—this is an important maxim that can also shape the Church of the future. The Church's call to synodality is a call to the entire world to see one another, and to begin to view the world differently. A synodal responsibility that is transferable to society is often exemplified in religious orders. Spirituality is a supporting pillar of this effort.

TRANSFORMATION CALLS FOR a realignment of life; it is also a springboard to the future. Allowing the one to be the other is the miracle of a life. Fortunately, we can refer to many wise individuals who have confronted this challenge and leave us with some insights we can follow.

The poet Basho writes, for example, "Do not seek to follow in the footsteps of the wise. Seek what they sought." And in his *Consolation of Philosophy*, the Roman philosopher Boethius teaches that every age that draws to an end is simply a new age coming to life. In other words, this does not mark the end of everything for either age.

The most important thing is to trust that the journey from one age to another can be life-giving on both sides—but in different ways. I, for example, at the age of eighty-six, am old enough to have lived between two ages and two Churches, and that is actually what I have done.

BETWEEN TWO CHURCHES: WHAT PERSPECTIVES DO THEY HAVE TO OFFER?

Each of the two Churches had something to offer. In the first Church—the older of the two—the main impression I had was of being in a well-managed institution. It was well-organized, clear in its expectations, certain of its teachings, universal in its norms, and narrowly defined by the ideas and behaviors that we had all acquired together. The aim of the endeavor was to achieve holiness by scaling each successive step with zeal and determination.

In point of fact, the need for performance and recognition was prevalent in the first of these two ages. If the way I led my life did not conform to the rules, to me, that felt like a shortcoming, loss, and guilt. The path to holiness became a private path marked out by participation in public events: baptism, confirmation, Sunday Mass, forty days of Lent, the four weeks of Advent, annual confession, Christmas, and Easter. These were the basic cornerstones for every pilgrim who diligently hewed to the path prescribed. It was a life full of "practices," all more a part of "trooping the color" than living an obligation to give one's life for others.

Some of us won all the prizes the first Church had to offer by following all the rules; the rest of us were more likely to be fellow travelers—true, one was in the midst of it all, but not entirely, and one was far less certain that the system itself was sacred. It came down to what I did based on the individual situation. It was not a matter of what the situation itself required of me in the process that led to my spiritual adulthood.

The second Church came much later in life—now, to be precise—at a time when the routine had long since lost both its appeal and its dynamism. Instead, spiritual life now invites us to live beyond the system and to answer the call of the Holy Spirit in each given moment. It feels like a fresh breeze. Like an opportunity. Like responsibility. Like love.

WHAT IS THE DIFFERENCE BETWEEN SPIRITUALISM AND SPIRITISM?

This path of the soul brings with it an invitation to new life, to nascent growth, to a constant new beginning. This is not so much about a routine that must be tackled over several levels as part of an effort to secure my ultimate salvation. Rather, it is a call to a life that I construct out of my heart and soul, for the good of the world around me and for my own growth in the here and now.

So where does the difference between the two Churches lie? The first path is a system built around established behaviors that are already considered "spiritual." Behaviors such as praying the rosary or abstaining from meat on Fridays. It comes about without the maturation of individual souls through the exertions of life or through the doing of good in the midst of altercations. This path lies between passive obedience to the system and the incapacitation of the adherents. Holiness, in this context, is deemed to consist in submission to the authorities. It is sincere and gives a public accounting for personal shortcomings. Although it attempts to do what our ancestors did, it does not succeed in liberating us so that we can understand life along the path, responding to it by shaping it together.

The second path, however, the new path, is a journey through life, characterized by compassion, justice, authenticity, and above all, responsibility. It is a path for pilgrims concerned with more than managing a calendar full of religious activities. This journey is the movement of the Catholic community through time for the good of the people it encounters along the way. It is through this journey that the arms of the Christian community open wide. It is through this journey that an affiliation occurs with those in the world whose own spirituality—Buddhist, Jewish, Muslim, Hindu—can unite proponents of peace and love, courage, and justice everywhere. They have all dedicated themselves to manifesting a healing presence everywhere along the way.

This journey of spiritual life is not about doing "spiritual things": things that, whether for reasons of personal piety or tradition, appear to be good to anyone whose heart is open to the world. It is about leading a spiritual life, a life that brings goodness and support to all those who need us along the way.

The "Synodal Path" of which Pope Francis speaks is a matter of creating human communion rather than retreating to our religious bunkers and ignoring life in general. It requires the authenticity of the Church: there is a vast difference between this stance, on the one hand, and obedience for its own sake on the other.

The words that Francis repeatedly uses to describe his vision of the Synodal Path are clear. He calls upon us to seek encounter, dialogue, a common path, open-mindedness and hospitality, bridge building, and tenderness.

He does not discuss Church policy or who has the say in a community in which clergy and the laity are on an equal footing, serving the whole world in an awareness of those who await the healing touch that we ourselves provide.

What is more, he certainly does not speak of a so-called spirituality that rests on incantations, invocations of unnatural beings, and the awakening of the dead. Those things are not "spirituality." This is "spiritism"—the calling-down of a series of unknown gods, potions, or miracles to fulfill our human desires.

THERE IS NO SYNODALITY WITHOUT SPIRITUALITY

Spirituality is the growth of the Christian consciousness that summons us to live as successors to Jesus, in a manner that the war-torn, desperate, poverty-stricken, racist, and sexist turmoil of our modern-day world requires.

Spirituality is companion to self-expression, a depth of spirit that leads us to new levels of spiritual understanding itself, to a deep and conscious spiritual life beyond the rules and habits that are observed for their own sake.

When Benedictine novices enter a monastery, straight away they are introduced to the practice of *lectio*—an in-depth, daily reflection on Holy Scripture, a word at a certain time, if necessary—as they struggle to discern what God wants of us in this place, with this communion and the openness it presents for the responsibility of the Christian community as well as of the individual Christian to take seriously the witness of the Church for the whole world and all its peoples.

How can this occur? Through my acknowledgment that the position and power of Christianity in the world is a function of the stance of the individual Christian. I am called upon to readily share my compassion, my dedication to justice, my authenticity, and my responsibility: this is nothing other than manifesting the presence of God's love. The way Jesus did.

They learn to remain silent as part of the search to find themselves and to recognize their own needs, to acknowledge and address their own struggles. At the same time, they begin to sense an obligation to the care of and commitment to the greater Benedictine community with which they will walk for the remainder of our shared lives, in love and embedded in the entire human community.

The question, of course, is how all this can happen when we come together as a group: as bishops, not as lords and masters; as priests who are brothers and not parish potentates; as men and women of religious orders who follow the charisma of their founders to enable all the gifts of Jesus to be brought to bear in the world; as healthy and happy laypeople, working in faith and modesty for the good of all in their families; as career professionals who also have a special spiritual gift and vocation; and as women who can finally contribute their own concerns, gifts, and insights into the ongoing development of the parish and the Church everywhere.

But how can this happen unless we ourselves become synodal members of the Universal Church, instead of looking on in disappointment at the turmoil of today's Church? The only way we can heal this turmoil is if we combine forces—if we are all prepared to touch the places where the pain is greatest.

WE CAN BE CHRISTIAN BEACONS

Without synodality, how can we find solace and security, if not in intentionally constituted groups moved by the Spirit, with the whole Church rising up, looking to tomorrow, filled with an awareness of the needs of the present, and ready to face them together?

A synodal Church rises as Christ did, so that the Spirit can continue to live in us—for our sake and for the sake of the entire world.

Imagine how this energy and this dedication would affect a world in waiting for the humanity it so desperately needs. Just imagine that for a moment!

Can this effort succeed? Of course it can. We can remember Basho and locate our own spirit of the past in the call of the present. From Boethius, we can learn that one age can lead another to wholeness. We can leave the wounds of the previous age behind us and proceed to build the new one—before it's too late.

We can become a Church, a community, a Christian beacon that illuminates the world so brightly that we ourselves are guided by it.

The Church's call to synodality is a call to the Church—to the world—to see one another, and to begin to view the world differently.

But to believe that the Catholic world can emerge from this World Synod in the same way in which we all went into it is not just a waste of time, but a waste of faith, hope and love.

Come, Lord Jesus, come!

NECESSARY PROCESSES OF REFORM

First Ecclesial Assembly of Latin America and the Caribbean

Birgit Weiler

Première for the Church of Latin America and the Caribbean: 2021 marked the first hybrid ecclesial assembly (*asamblea eclesial*) held in Mexico. It was the product of a two-year process during which the different voices of the people of God were heard and included in different ways. The report offers a first-hand account of the experiences shared and topics advanced at the assembly.

THE INTENTION OF THE Episcopal Conference of Latin America (CELAM) to promote synodality in the Church of Latin America and the Caribbean was fulfilled in November 2021. This marked the first time in the history of the continent that an ecclesial (and not just an episcopal!) assembly could be held for Latin America and the Caribbean. In preparation for the Assembly, for the first time, the Church implemented a broad process of mutual listening (*Proceso de escucha*) throughout the region. Never before had the voices of the people of God, in their great diversity, been sought so widely.

These are the voices of young people, of different generations of men and women, of members of native peoples and peoples of African heritage, of small farmers, of people in a variety of urban settings, of students, of members of the LGTBIQ communities and associations, of people with disabilities, of Christians from churches not affiliated with Rome, and also of those who define themselves as nonbelievers in the religious sense of the term.

There was a concerted determination to include all those who would not otherwise rank among the usual interlocutors in the various ecclesial circles, and people who generally have little to no relationship with the Catholic Church: people of goodwill throughout the various movements of civil society. Unfortunately, however, the pandemic left only very limited scope in which to secure the participation of people at the periphery of society, and specifically to hear their voices—voices that are generally barely heard, if at all.

CLERICALISM: AN OBSTACLE TO A SYNODAL CHURCH

In all, more than seventy thousand people took part in the process. With some 425 million Catholics in Latin America, the merits of the participation that the listening process generated are clear, but further efforts are needed to hear from far more people along the path to a Synodal Church. Numerous people in Peru took part in this as well. As in other countries, working commissions at the various ecclesial levels in that country were important places of learning for the synodality that accompanies the process. There were solid learning processes in place in many cases—processes that are still there—including joining together in a communal and fraternal spirit, and consulting and deciding with one another—laypeople, men and women of religious orders, priests and bishops. Over the course of the listening process, some topics were put forward particularly emphatically.

First among these was clericalism as one of the most powerful obstacles to a Synodal Church. The many commentaries on the subject included the observation that clericalism was closely linked to the abuse of power. Quite a few contributions note that a clerical structure "completely minimizes" the role of the laity in the Church and deprives women and men of "the opportunity to develop their vocation." Many share the observation made by Pope Francis that clericalism constitutes one of the most severe deformations and distortions of the Catholic Church in Latin America and consequently must urgently be overcome.

Moreover, as was repeatedly pointed out, a clerical attitude and style of thinking can now be seen among many laypeople and members of religious orders as well. This is why a fraternal Church requires a shared commitment to a renunciation of clerical attitudes, practices, and ways of thinking. On this topic, there is such division, in the minds of Latin Americans, that nothing less than fidelity to the gospel and the credibility of the Church are at stake.

As was underscored at the first Ecclesial Assembly, the effort to follow Jesus requires us to break free of relationship patterns that are associated with the abuse of power, domination over others, and authoritarian practices. It challenges us to keep a living memory of the words of Jesus, in which je singles out and sharply criticizes the abuse of power by the powerful of his time: "Not so among you" (Mark 10:43; par. Matt 20:26). For it is much more in keeping with the Spirit of Jesus to establish relationships on an equal footing, based on mutual respect and mutual appreciation for the vocation and gifts of others—in an awareness that baptism made us all sisters and brothers in the faith and gave us the gift of God's Spirit.

Various articles highlight the importance of courage in personally and collectively opening oneself to power of the Holy Spirit (*audacia*) that seeks to lead the Church on new paths of conversion and transformation. For many of those who have taken part in the entire process of the Ecclesial

Assembly, this time is a *kairos* that requires openness and determination on our parts in the context of needed processes of reform in the Church.

Various contributions in the listening process address the fact that many congregations in Latin America have small numbers of young people who are continuously engaged. Many young people, when coming into contact with a congregation, initially take a genuine interest in participating in various activities in the context of pastoral care of the youth. Not infrequently, though, they distance themselves in frustration after some time as they do not experience open-minded, dynamic, and interactive pastoral care that responds to the realities, fears, and hopes of their lives.

In an Open Letter during the Ecclesial Assembly of Latin America and the Caribbean, the youth representatives said that the path to a synodal Church must necessarily include giving young people greater scope for action in the Church. They need to become much more involved in the committees and executive bodies in which questions about the Church and pastoral care are discussed and decided together.

JUST PARTICIPATION AND SHARING FOR WOMEN IN THE CHURCH

On the part of many women and men, including bishops and priests, the demand for comprehensive ecclesial reforms as part of the effort to achieve fair participation and sharing for women in the Church was also very evident in many of the contributions to the listening process. The vast majority of active members of the Church in Latin America and the Caribbean are women. In many places throughout the region, the presence and vitality of the Church is due to the strong commitment of women in the various areas of pastoral care; many women are in charge of congregations that are rarely visited by priests.

Significantly, in spite of the high number of women who are dedicated to serving the Church, only a relatively small number of them are in positions of ecclesiastical leadership. It was often stated that it is essential for a synodal Church to overcome the patriarchal mentality and asymmetries of power in the Church; to create greater gender justice; and to work resolutely to ensure that women are involved as far as possible in the composition and leadership of the commissions and committees in which decisions of sweeping significance are taken with regard to pastoral care, mission, finances, and the administration of the Church. Several strong comments were heard voicing the concern to boldly advance the topic of ministries and offices for women in the Church, including the Women's diaconate.

The cases of abuse in the Church of Latin America were addressed as well. Multiple voices were heard expressing indignation and pain over sexual abuse as well as the abuse of conscience and power on the part of priests and other members of the Church. The contributions express profound concern for the suffering inflicted on the victims, minors in particular. There is a call for the Church in Latin America to cease the concealment and cover-up of cases of abuse, and to acknowledge instead that a serious problem exists.

Provision must also be made for transparency, justice, and reparations in a holistic sense, along with effective measures to prevent abuse. It is considered a sign of hope that reliable processes have already been set in motion in various local churches in the effort to prevent abuse while ensuring transparent procedures along with justice and redress for the victims. At the same time, it is emphasized that these are only the first steps on a long path.

In Peru, following the Ecclesial Assembly, the Bishops' Conference set up a working commission at the national level. Its task is to coordinate with local churches to encourage and assist with the step-by-step implementation of decisions, reforms, and pastoral orientations. This is done in cooperation with the Working Commission for the World Synod. An interest in international exchange can be found throughout Latin America. This exchange is already in place in some respects: in the area of preventing and addressing abuse in the Church, for example, or around questions about the role of women in the Church. In the Church of Latin America and the Caribbean, we are currently experiencing a dynamic process of transition and renewal in the Spirit of God. Along our synodal path, the word of God as related by the Prophet Isaiah serves as a source of inspiration: "I am about to do a new thing; now it springs forth, do you not perceive it?" (Isa 43:19).

TOWARD A UNIVERSAL PHILOSOPHY OF SYNODALITY

Christina Kheng

Synodal leadership? What seems paradoxical at first sight is, in the Asian context, a pastoral vision for the future of the Church. Synodality involves the profound mystery of being in relationship with God and each other, in mutual self-giving, authenticity, openness, vulnerability, with trust and discernment, and in gradual maturing through the vicissitudes of life. Dialogue between Church and society is indispensable in this.

BEING A UNIVERSAL CHURCH on the move entails ongoing dialogue about the signs of the times. This includes not just current trends in every culture and context but also developments in each field of human knowledge. One particular field that has been gaining increased interest in the Catholic Church is that of leadership and management. Since the early 2000s, there has been a growth of degree programs, training workshops, pastoral literature, and consultancy services aimed at enhancing leadership and management in the Church.

A spectrum of reasons has been cited for this, ranging from the personal and systemic issues highlighted by the clergy sexual abuse crisis to the rising expectations for professionalism in ministry and the need to better manage resources. Now the emphasis on synodality has brought even more attention to the topic of pastoral leadership and how it might be reconceived. While this has sparked new interest in the synodal approach to leadership, not a few pastors are experiencing a sense of uncertainty. If all the people of God are coresponsible for the life and mission of the Church, and all are called to walk together side by side, what then is the role of pastoral leaders? For the clergy in particular, how do they exercise their priestly vocation in an "inverted pyramid"? This image has become widely associated with a synodal Church after it was used by Pope Francis in a speech commemorating the fiftieth anniversary of the Synod of Bishops. Since then, it has been associated with the notion of a synodal Church.

Some Church leaders have responded by demonstrating either of two extremes—reasserting a top-down authority in the name of ensuring orderliness and fidelity to the faith tradition or withdrawing almost completely in the name of letting the laity take charge. Neither response is in line with the principle of synodality.

WHERE IS THE GOLDEN MEAN?

Between these two extremes, there are those who are endeavoring to find a middle way. This might include dialoguing, facilitating, guiding, empowering, directing, consulting, and jointly moving forward. To this end, there is increasing recognition that advances in the social sciences might help address gaps in ecclesial skills and formation. More Church organizations now have their eyes on tools, especially in the leadership and organization fields.

Indeed, a plethora of tools exist to facilitate teamwork, communication, consensus building, joint decision-making, restructuring for collaboration, and even ethical and spiritual leadership. In this regard, the tradition of the Catholic faith has affirmed the potential presence of truth in all human disciplines under certain conditions, as well as their relevance to the life and mission of the Church. Nevertheless, theologians and management scholars alike have cautioned about the ways in which social science tools can reinforce epistemologies, worldviews, and anthropologies that are fragmented, secularist, empiricist, self-seeking, and Pelagian.

Indeed, throughout the history of the Judeo-Christian tradition, the people of God have borrowed from sociopolitical and organizational systems of their contemporaneous societies and experienced both positive and negative consequences. Even now, there are those who insist that the litmus test of the Church's synodality rests on whether a wide range of people are allowed to exercise democratic votes at synodal assemblies.

Does synodality really boil down to these extrinsic mechanisms? Perhaps such views reflect the tendency once again to espouse contemporaneous social paradigms without sufficient reflexivity and discernment.

There is a need to critically examine our ways of proceeding and their underlying assumptions especially at the level of philosophical foundations. Specifically, what role does faith play in these foundations? The Church cannot assert that its teaching on synodality is far superior to secular views about participation and democratic leadership. However, it does have a message to offer, which is at the heart of the Church's very nature and existence.

This message is that the trinitarian God creates and calls humankind—and indeed the whole cosmos—to be in a dynamic and ever-growing communion of love. Such communion has an eschatological dimension that directs the human gaze toward eternity. At the same time, divine grace is ever active to make this communion a reality in the temporal order. Human beings are invited to cooperate with this grace and participate in the divine life of self-giving love as they traverse together through history.

A UNIVERSAL FOUNDATION FOR SYNODALITY IS NEEDED

Thus synodality and synodal leadership are much more than mechanisms for democratic participation. They involve the deep mystery of being in relationship with God and one another in mutual self-giving, authenticity, openness, trust, vulnerability, discernment, and gradual maturation through the vicissitudes of life. For the present world affected by division, individualism, secularism, abuse of power, and overemphasis on instantaneity and control, this message brings much hope and encouragement even as it is countercultural.

Going forward, an integral part of the Church's mission today might be to engage with society in jointly discovering a universal philosophy of synodality and its consequent practicalities for synodal leadership. In this regard, when it comes to interdisciplinary dialogue, such as when a religious tradition is brought together with the secular sciences and culture, the issue of methodology warrants attention. This is because the method we apply, whether deliberately or unconsciously, manifests our underlying stances about truth, revelation, and human knowing.

No single body of knowledge within the secular sciences, culture, or religious teaching can be taken as an absolute orienting principle for all the other disciplines. This is not only because each is different in focus but also because no discipline is without internal debates and divergences nor room for further development toward truth.

Hence a basic and normative foundation needs to be established through common discernment. Admittedly, such an effort is not easy as it requires a collective confrontation with fundamental questions on the principle of existence, and consequently what is ultimately true, good, and valuable. This demands time, space, and openness to listening, sharing, reflecting, praying or contemplating, and then possibly changing one's paradigms.

UNDERSTANDING THE DIVISION OF DUTIES AS A SHARED RESPONSIBILITY

Nevertheless, the fruit of such effort is a common philosophy of synodality that can promote the fraternity of humankind and indeed, the integral ecology of all the cosmos. As a pilgrim people, the Church and all of humanity are called to ongoing transformation toward fullness of life even while they negotiate new times and contexts. This implies ongoing clarification of what is truly essential and enduring, and what is variable or in need of change and adaptation. The *ressourcement* and *aggiornamento* consequently need to be guided by a compass of foundational beliefs. As a starting point for reflection, a universal philosophy of synodality might be expressed in terms of an intrinsic bond between all humankind and the cosmos, uniting them in a common life and shared sense of being. This might be palpable in people's experience of the local and global community, even as it is fraught with division.

Divine love, which could be encountered by people without religious affiliation as a gratuitous and universal potential of goodness and solidarity, is present everywhere in the world, vivifying its communion and flourishing. Such flourishing is developmental and multidimensional and includes the material, social, cultural, mental, and spiritual. Moreover, humanity participates freely in this movement, each one bringing diverse gifts to bear, and collaborating together in attentiveness to the divine flow.

With this foundation, the roles of human leadership within the Church might be identified. They would include promoting communal growth in faith and discernment, encouraging each person's development, facilitating fruitful collaboration toward universal flourishing, animating relationships of fraternal love, and ensuring fidelity to enduring values whilst promoting relevance to current contexts. These roles could be regarded as the shared responsibility of the whole community even while they are distributed in accord with each one's giftedness.

Additionally, the above view of a foundation for synodality elucidates some criteria by which secular leadership tools as well as current ecclesial practices can be assessed. For instance, we could ask the following questions: To what extent are they premised on and do they promote the intrinsic connectedness of people, communities, and the whole cosmos? To what extent do they promote universal flourishing in all dimensions, including the holistic development and vocation of every person? To what extent do they espouse an eschatological horizon, and acknowledge the limitations of the temporal order and its developmental nature? To what extent do they promote human cooperation with the divine initiative and the attendant spirituality?

These principles could serve as basic orientations for the role of leadership in a synodal Church and society. It can be seen that they entail more than the learning of new knowledge and skills, important as these are. Rather, they call for a deepening of the interior life, including an authentic life of faith and a wholehearted embrace of community. Only then can there be genuine dialogue among all sectors in Church and society, and a commitment to walk together in humility and love.

FINDING ORIENTATION IN FAITH: HERE AND NOW

The theological foundations of the Synodal Path

Thomas Söding

Turn around and make a new start. This is what the Synodal Path of the Catholic Church in Germany wants. An "orientation text" was adopted as the first document. The theological net it spans is both a reason for reform and an invitation.

THE CATHOLIC CHURCH has great potential to set out in search of orientation at any time and in any place: What does God's Spirit say to the congregations? How can the word of God be understood and proclaimed here and now? How can the insights of faith be combined with social responsibility and the cultural characteristics of Christianity?

CHURCH AS GLOBAL PRAYER

If this potential is to be realized, one-sidedness must be overcome: as if only the pope and the bishops had something to say in the Church, or as if theology sought to establish an expertocracy, or as if the majority opinion of a single nation were the measure of all things. Overcoming the one-sidedness and tapping into this potential is based on a self-critical as well as self-confident, an informed as well as engaged clarification: where, when, and how the convictions of faith are formed, and where questions of faith are asked and discoveries of faith can be made.

Answering these questions in a differentiated way is more important than ever before. The Catholic Church is a living organism; it is an ancient institution with a great future; it is the only *global player* that is also a *global prayer*. That is why it has a vast store of experiences, such as achieving reforms, creating images, and achieving impacts.

Yet it is undergoing a structural crisis worldwide—a crisis that is essentially a spiritual one. The abuse of spiritual power poisons the communion of the Church. The contradictions between traditional notions and fresh perspectives from the natural, human, and cultural sciences are tearing many believers apart. Conspiracy theories against the "Zeitgeist" do not stop at Church walls and are even espoused by individual Church princes.

This crisis is the downside of a great opportunity. If membership in the Church is not a matter of course, faith can develop in the freedom characteristic to it. If there are appealing alternatives, what matters is to indicate the reasons for the Church—reasons without which it would not exist. When old thought patterns are no longer convincing, it is time to turn around and attempt a new beginning. This is what the Statutes of the Synodal Path say. This is why it is necessary to initiate a synodal process throughout the Catholic Church, as the invitation by Pope Francis shows.

The Synodal Path in Germany is focused on topics deriving directly from the scientific investigation of abuse by members of the clergy: power and separation of powers, images of priests, women's rights, and sexual morality. The path is the responsibility not of the bishops alone but the shared responsibility with the lay organization of German Catholicism, the ZdK (Central Committee of German Catholics). No one disputes that there are far more questions that require answering in a synodal fashion. But if there are systemic causes for abuse and its cover-up, then systemic solutions are needed if the Catholic Church is to be in a position to listen and speak again.

Basic theological questions arise across all of the thematic fields, questions that are not purely theoretical in nature but of high practical relevance instead. While they do not touch upon the foundations of dogma, they do require a review of established habits. Along this path, the bishops are far more involved in the deliberations and decision-making processes of the entire people of God than the Catholic Church has been accustomed to since the Vatican Councils.

That is why the Synodal Path has shown that it is good to write an "orientation text" that makes the theological approach transparent, so that situations can be analyzed accurately, with correctly assessed alternatives and logically drawn consequences. This orientation text has been favorably received, not least by the ecumenical community; but it has also provoked criticism, not least from conservatives.

The orientation-text approach is deeply rooted in the Catholic Church: no false alternatives, but genuine relationships; no monotony, but polyphony; no stagnation, but movement. An important point of reference is the doctrine of *loci theologici*, the "places" of theology. It is not enshrined in the counterreformatory ambition of a *Melchior Cano*; instead, as Pope Francis emphasizes, it is provided with a time index—as history does not stop, but goes on, and God's Spirit does not nurture nostalgia, but inspires constant renewal. The image is not that of a pyramid, where one figure at the pinnacle would determine everything, but that of a net, as cast by the fishermen at the Sea of Galilee. No "place" exists in isolation; each is the junction of a greater whole that functions when it coheres.

IN FIRST PLACE: HOLY SCRIPTURE

In the first place, there is Holy Scripture: not as a dead letter or paper pope but as a human witness to the word of God, rooted in the history of Israel, inspired by Jesus, and sustained by the mission of the young Church. Scripture goes hand in hand with the tradition that already shaped the Bible but that, in every generation, is measured against Holy Scripture, so that it does not ossify but develops dynamically instead. Scripture and tradition are established "places" of theology. But biblicalism is as bad as traditionalism. The Bible must be interpreted and the tradition filled with life. Everyone is called upon, with different tasks.

The orientation text takes its inspiration from Pope John XXIII, who discerns "signs of the times," such as the women's movement and the trade-union movement, as an indicator of God's role in the present. This term is used more openly at times in the Pastoral Constitution *Gaudium et Spes*; in this usage, it represents all those ambivalent phenomena of the day that have not yet been put to the test of reason and faith that permits a distinction among the spirits involved. In some cases, however, the Council also determines the specific meaning that the orientation text adopts: signs of the times can also be situated outside of the Church, as signs of the Spirit.

The sciences and the arts, the ecological movement, human rights, and peace policy: with the aid of all of these, the Church learns to understand the gospel better. It is not above reviewing and modifying its own convictions in dialogue with the "world" if to do so proves necessary.

INTUITION AND VOICE OF THE PEOPLE OF GOD

On the other hand, it is undisputed that the "sense of faith" of the people of God is a *locus theologicus*. What is under dispute, however, is how it can be identified. Under traditional models, it can only be recognized by virtue of its assent to the magisterium. In 2014, however, the International Theological Commission clarified that it is also proactive: there is an intuition of the people of God—an intuition of what is timely and when the magisterium exceeds its bounds or theology has gone off track. This sense of faith is not easy—but not impossible—to discern. All of the executive bodies must develop a sensorium: *vox populi vox Dei.*

If they are more than mere assemblies of bishops, synods are the best places in which to voice the faith of the people of God—not in a single language, but in all the mother tongues of this world. Creating forums devoted to the sense of faith, in both digital and analog form: there is nearly no more daunting task today, nearly no task is approached with less consistency. That is what makes fundamentalisms and hate speech proliferate in areas in which it would be important to give voice to the Catholic faith, in a spirit of ecumenical fraternity.

Magisterium and theology remain. They weaken each other if they view themselves as opponents. The two can grow together if they respect each other. The magisterium relieves theology of the task of depicting the unity of the Church; the task of theology is to examine traditions and to think about alternatives. It must be free to do so, especially in research, but it does not have that freedom at present.

MAGISTERIUM AND THEOLOGY

Theology relieves the magisterium of the obligation to lose itself in details of interpretation and application, an area in which it has no competence anyway; the task of the magisterium is to bear witness to the simple and liberating truth of faith—thus, above all, serving the simple members of the Church, the poor in particular. Wherever bans on teaching have been instituted, the magisterium is not quite itself and has essentially come up short for having failed to keep an open conversation about faith—apart from the fact that the legal procedures are inadequate and teaching bans often have limited half-lives.

The orientation text of the Synodal Path in Germany was not written in the "spirit of cowardice" but in a spirit "of power and of love and of self-discipline" (2 Tim 1:7). This is how the presidents of the Synodal Path introduced the text; following thorough discussion and intense debate, the members of the Synodal Assembly then approved it by an overwhelming majority. More than 70 percent of the German bishops were in concurrence.

Not all of the applications and specifications can be derived from the theological foundations. And yet the orientation text serves as a matrix for theological argumentation. It offers an instance of intellectual honesty and spiritual responsibility in public. It also serves as an invitation to the entire Catholic Church to set off on a path, in search of orientation in faith: here and today, for there and tomorrow.

"WE CANNOT NOT BE SYNODAL"

A conversation with Cardinal Mario Grech, Secretary General of the Synod of Bishops

Cardinal Mario Grech with Anna Mertens

Cardinal Mario Grech, General Secretary of the Synod, expresses satisfaction and gratitude for the great commitment of those around the world who are helping to shape the future of the Church and make synodality a living experience. The focus is on "staying on the track of God's will." Trust in the German Synod Way is intact.

I have to be honest with you, I find it very difficult to explain to anyone what synodality means. Can you help me?

Cardinal Mario Grech: Synod means "walking together." In his encyclical *Fratelli Tutti*, Pope Francis points out that we live in a culture marked by profound individualism and that we must respond to people who are tired of walking alone. Synodality is the opposite, it means "walking together" and is a constitutive dimension of the Church. In the Church there is no room for individualism.

We are the people of God, called to be a community. Inviting us to be more synodal, the Holy Father is telling us to recomprehend what "people of God" really means. If we rediscover our relationships to create a more communal spirit, that would be a great step forward. Not only in the Church.

In this sense the Synod for a synodal Church is just a start of a long, an eternal process?

Grech: The Synod is the kickstart. It is an opportunity to reflect on the need to become more synodal as a Church. And to discover new ways to be more synodal and to strengthen those we already practice to make them more effective.

This process has started. Are you happy with its start and its progress?

Grech: Yes, the signals we are getting from various parts of the world are positive. I think we are on the right track. As an example, I've just been to Lebanon and I was surprised by the amount of enthusiasm. If you ask me whether all are on board: no. Some dioceses are hesitant. But I haven't lost hope. Gradually, they will join the process. After all, synodality is not an agenda or some extra work. It is our nature as a Church. We cannot not be synodal.

You have provided the dioceses with documents and guidelines.

Grech: Our ministry is not to dictate, but to accompany. We want to help our brothers and sisters to "walk the talk" and for this we have provided materials that can serve to stimulate the process. We have an idea; we are making progress and we are on a good path. Some say we have already written our final document. That's not true. We started from a blank sheet of paper and slowly we are writing it together. And what is even more important are the relationships and ties that, through the synodal process, are being created at all levels.

Have you already received or read contributions from different dioceses?

Grech: So far we have received responses from a number of Bishops' Conferences: the deadline for submission is mid-August. And we have also received a decent number of individual contributions. This is a possibility, too. However, we encourage all to submit their contribution to the local Churches because the universal Church exists in and from the particular Churches.

What is your next step?

Grech: As soon as we have received and read the responses received from the Bishops' Conferences and other stakeholders (Eastern Churches, religious congregations, dicasteries of the Roman Curia), our first task will be to prepare the working document to serve the continental phase of the synodal process. In the past, the General Secretariat of the Synod would entrust just few theologians with the drafting of this document. This time, however, we have decided to appoint a group of around thirty experts from around the world. Together we will retreat for fifteen days to analyze all the proposals and prepare the document for the next phase. It will be a synodal and spiritual experience.

Have you chosen the members already?

Grech: Yes, from all over the world and different backgrounds. Men and women, of course. Most are already involved in the synodal process. We asked them for their willingness to read the materials received before we met and to prepare a summary highlighting the elements that struck them most.

And after that?

Grech: Once this document has been approved, it will be forwarded to all bishops. We will ask all bishops to convene diocesan synod leaders to reflect on the document in preparation for the continental stage. Then there will be Continental Synodal Assemblies taking place next year from January to March. We are planning to have seven continental meetings. I have set up a task force that will accompany these meetings. You will be able to follow these steps on our website www.synod.va.

How many people work in the Secretariat for the Synod?

Grech: We are only fourteen. But I have set up four commissions: theological, spiritual, methodological, and one for communication, all in all seventy to eighty people. And they are all very generous and willing to help us.

What's the feedback you're getting from within the curia?

Grech: There has not yet been a meeting with the whole curia, but we have tried to visit all dicasteries. The general response has been quite positive. All the dicasteries are invited to submit their contribution to the consultative phase. I am also aware that some dicasteries are conducting a synodal process in their offices, involving all staff.

On your travels have there always been the same issues brought to your attention?

Grech: I didn't enter into details with the people I met. Sometimes there are lists of topics. When I travel, I try to listen and to encourage and in turn I am also encouraged a lot. More than anything, I feel that there is a great enthusiasm for the Synod.

Why? Because they feel heard?

Grech: Yes, they appreciate that they have one more opportunity to make their voices heard. And this about a particular theme: for a synodal Church. I expect, there will be contributions that address other issues, but the main issue is "a synodal Church." I believe that once we're more synodal, we will also be in a better position to address other issues.

What if there is no feedback? If a diocese doesn't want to participate?

Grech: This can happen. I have, for instance, received a letter informing us that in a particular diocese the bishop is not convinced and is not organizing the process. But the nuncio in this country was clever enough to address the faithful directly and encouraged them to hand their contributions to him. All of us are asked to contribute, no one is excluded.

Let's have a look at the German synodal path, which has been going on for quite some time. There have been preliminary results, have they been presented to you?

Grech: No, nobody has officially presented the preliminary results to us. But I understand that. Until the 5th of June when the Apostolic Constitution on the reform of the Roman curia *Praedicate Evangelium* came into force, we were the "General Secretariat for the Synod of Bishops," and in this sense not responsible for a synodal assembly. Only now we are the "General Secretariat for the Synod." That is more than a change of names.

Have you read the results obtained to date?

Grech: I try to follow the process. But for me, it is one thing to follow what is published and another thing to follow what actually happens. It is a process. Perhaps the communication in general could have been better and that would have helped a better understanding of what happens in Germany. I have trust in the Catholic Church in Germany, in the bishops, and I trust they know what they are doing.

You have been formally invited to go to Germany by Bishop Gregor Batzing. Have you planned your trip already?

Grech: Not yet. I was formally invited, but back then, it wasn't possible for me to go.

And are you going to go anytime soon?

Grech: I don't rule it out.

Is something stopping you from going there?

Grech: No, absolutely not. I am in good and regular contact with Bishop Georg Batzing.

What topics would you like to discuss with the members of the German synodal path?

Grech: I do not feel it's appropriate to enter in an ongoing discussion. The same applies to the synodal plenary council in Australia. We have to respect the local Churches. If we're asked for assistance, that's something else. I would probably stress the general principle of synodality in the Catholic Church. There is the reciprocal listening of the people of God—all included—then there is collegiality. Every bishop is part of the college of bishops. And there is Peter—the principle of unity and certainty. Those three levels have to be respected—always.

There has been criticism about the German synodal path from different Churches, such as Poland. Do you know why?

Grech: I cannot say why there has been such criticism. But I am puzzled over the method and the style used by the critics. I think a fraternal correction and dialogue are something very positive. But why a public denunciation? It seems to me that it does not help. It only creates more polarization.

Have you seen similar controversies in other countries regarding other synodal paths, for example, in Australia?

Grech: I have the impression that certain issues that are being discussed in Germany are also being discussed elsewhere. But again, there are different ways of discussing those topics. Let me try to explain myself with an example. I had just taken office and one of the first letters I received was from a bishop who had just concluded a diocesan synodal process. He wrote me that before he started the process, he had told his diocese that certain topics couldn't be discussed within the process because it wasn't within his competence as a diocesan bishop to address them. But in the end the people discussed them no matter what. So, he asked me whether he should disregard those topics or include them in the final document. I told him to stand by what he had stated at the beginning but without disregarding or discarding those topics. I told him to write another document, such as an appendix, and submit it to the higher authority.

Do you know what the response was in the diocese?

Grech: No, but I have the impression the community took it well. Because the bishop listened. Questions are not only important, but necessary. What really worries me is when there are no questions. Questions mean we are alive and continue to develop.

Do there have to be results that change things at the end of a synodal process?

Grech: The main goal of this process is to find God's will and better understand it. And 2020 is not 1020, nor is it 2000. So, we have to be faithful to God. At the same time, we have to find the right answers for the people today.

Part II
GLOBAL PERSPECTIVES

RE-ENABLING THE PROCLAMATION OF THE GOSPEL

Germany

Franz-Josef Bode

Rising from a situation of profound crisis, the Church in Germany has set out on the Synodal Path. This source reveals a basic orientation as a path of conversion and renewal.

THE TRIGGER EVENT FOR the Synodal Path is what was referred to as the "MHG Study" (Mannheim, Heidelberg, Giesen Study), which was issued in 2018. The publication of this scholarly work, commissioned by the German bishops in an effort to explore in greater detail the causes for the numerous cases of sexual violence against minors and their cover-up in the Catholic Church, led to a fresh sense of deep upheaval. The publication identified numerous shortcomings and faults in Church structures. The study addressed a host of immediate aspects and indications for use in addressing these wrongs and preventing their recurrence, together with further, systemic issues.

The German Bishops' Conference then addressed the topics of "The use of power in the Church," "The future of the profession and image of priests," and "Further development of Catholic sexual morality" during the study day of its Spring General Assembly in Lingen, Germany, in 2019. The bishops agreed that far-reaching steps would be required to address the problems shown, to renew the Church and thus restore a credible space in which the gospel could flourish. The Central Committee of German Catholics (ZdK) was immediately prepared to play an active role in the process that lay ahead.

FULL VOTING RIGHTS FOR ALL STAKEHOLDERS: SYNODALITY IN AN EMERGENCY

Right from the outset, it was clear that this path had to lead to concrete results and practical consequences. The ZdK also urged that the topic of "Women in the Church" be included as a top priority in the process. Soon it was evident that the external form of a synod, in the sense of a canonical plenary council, would present difficulties, as it would necessitate longer preparation, and joint consultations and decision-making on an equal footing would not be terribly easy to implement. Synodality was thus to be enacted in a manner that would permit full voting rights for all stakeholders. Hence, the decision was taken to set out on a Synodal Path that on the one hand affords participation by many dedicated individuals and the involvement of existing expertise, while on the other hand not circumventing or even undermining the ecclesiologically and canonically indispensable decision-making authority of the bishops.

CONSTRUCTIVELY AND COURAGEOUSLY CONFRONTING THE CRISIS OF THE CHURCH

The inspiration that arose out of the MHG Study, and the approach taken to deal with the systemic sources and cover-up of abuse, are inseparable from the basic situation and the discussions of ecclesial reform that have been ongoing for many years. At the beginning of the twenty-first century, the Church is undoubtedly faced with great challenges and problems, as suggested in catchphrases as in the sharp decline in popular ecclesiality, the loss of the matter-of-factness of the Christian faith, the shortage of priests and the growing distance between the faithful and the Church.

The discussion process carried out within the Church in Germany between 2011 and 2015 and known as "Believe in Today" (*Im Heute glauben*) was an initial attempt along the path toward an open-minded and constructive consideration of these questions that have been put before the Church. This was a first step, showing that the Church must adopt a more courageous approach to reforms, even in the face of obstruction, if it wants to take seriously its mission of credibly proclaiming the Gospel of Jesus Christ to people today.

The Synodal Path is a path of conversion and renewal, as is stated explicitly at the beginning of its Statutes. It is characterized by an awareness of the Church's individual and structural failure to deal with sexualized violence. But it is also sustained by the certainty that the Church can be re-formed, renewed from the core of its being.

Through this concern, a structure of the Synodal Path was developed that brings great commitment and expertise to the effort to address the topics involved in the MHG Study, developing them further in ways that lead to practical change. Along with the Synodal Assembly as a comprehensive deliberative body, this is why the four Synodal Forums also have an important role to play. Under considerations of "Power and the separation of powers in the Church," "Priestly existence today," "Women in ministries and offices in the Church," and "Life in successful relationships," these forums afford analysis of systemic problems, discuss possible reforms, examine their feasibility and the level of action required and compose all of this in the form of texts introduced during the Synodal Assembly.

GUIDING PERSPECTIVES THAT POINT THE WAY FOR OUR WORK TOGETHER

The overarching guiding perspectives for the Synodal Path include the following aspects in particular: the Church is the community of those who have accepted the gospel of Jesus Christ, conduct their lives based on this, and know how to go forth and proclaim this gospel. A shadow is cast upon this witness by the guilt and the sin that individual Christians, and the Church as a whole, must bear. The harm of sexual violence, and of efforts to cover it up, is a quintessential example of this sin and calls for repentance. While the German Bishops' Conference makes every effort to provide concrete information about and ways to address abuse in a variety of contexts and through a variety of projects, the Synodal Path is primarily concerned with gaining new trust among people through systemic reforms and by bolstering proclamation of the gospel.

As far as the search for new approaches is concerned, it is indispensable to affirm, over and over again, the *sources* of ecclesiastical activity. Anyone who seeks to understand, accept, enact, and proclaim the gospel will also need to engage in interpretation, conversation, and adaptation. Here, biblical sources are supplemented by the tradition of the Church, statements by the Church's magisterium, the reflections of theology, the sense of faith of all the faithful, and, not least, the signs of the times. It is in these that scientific knowledge, for example, can be understood as inspiration toward a deeper understanding of the gospel.

That the active participation of the faithful is indispensable to the Church contrasts with the fact that many among them feel excluded from the Church's decision-making processes. For this and for many other reasons, they are growing more and more distanced and alienated. This makes *participation* an urgent concern of the Synodal Path—meaning both the possibility of always taking part in decisions as well as the specific willingness to cooperate and commit. This is why the synodal structures must be developed further across all levels of ecclesial activity.

IN CONSTANT INTERACTION WITH THE UNIVERSAL CHURCH

Even before the Synodal Path began, it was clear that many of the concerns and topics addressed here could not be clarified or even instituted at the individual-church level. So it is important to always look closely to see what can be accomplished locally, promptly and in specific ways, and what kinds of concerns must be introduced to the discourse of the Universal Church.

It was with this in mind that, from the outset, the German bishops sought dialogue with Pope Francis and the dicasteries of the Holy See. In contact with bishops and Catholics all over the world, the Synodals are also serious about the call by Pope Francis, as he stated it in his letter, "To the pilgrim people of God in Germany": to enter into *communion with the Universal Church* and to seek a candid answer to the current situation. That he invited the entire Universal Church to a common Synodal Path with a view to the Synod of Bishops in 2023 also affords an opportunity to network the concerns of local Churches with the discourse that is ongoing worldwide.

The Synodal Path is a *profoundly spiritual event.* In celebrating the Eucharist, in prayer and in the reading of the Scriptures, we repeatedly seek the assistance of the Holy Spirit. The Church in Germany, like the Church around the world, depends on this to such a great extent. As members of the Synodal Assembly, we hope that we are on the right path.

WHEN CRISES GIVE RISE TO NEW THINGS

Switzerland

Daniel Kosch

The Synodal Path in Germany has long since become more than a self-contained process of reform. It sets standards and brings courage and hope to many local Churches. As neighboring countries in particular are demonstrating, synodal principles and decisive steps are important. Depending on the context involved, different synodal paths may be required.

THREE THINGS WERE PRESENT when the Synodal Path for the Catholic Church in Germany began: first, there was the vision of Pope Francis that God expects the Church of the third millennium to pursue a "path of synodality"; a second factor involved the analysis of the crisis of abuse, which pointed up fundamental questions that the Church must ask itself: its approach to power, its relationship to human sexuality, and questions of the things that constitute offices and the position of women in the Church; a third element concerned the realization that breathing life into the vision of a synodal Church and managing the crisis of abuse require a joint approach by the Bishops' Conference and the Central Committee of German Catholics (ZdK).

Like the majority of the laity engaged in the Church in Switzerland, I, too, have a vision of a synodal Church—based on the view that the Church is deep in a crisis—and a conviction that the Church is in need of profound reforms. In 2019, it was with these thoughts in mind that I viewed the announcement of the Synodal Path in our neighbor, Germany, as an important sign of hope. And when, a short time later, bishops in Switzerland also acknowledged the "crisis" facing the Church, announcing a "synodal approach" in response, I held hopes that a process of reforms would be launched in Switzerland as well.

A NECESSARY AND DEMANDING PROJECT ROOTED IN THE COURAGE OF FAITH

The course that the Synodal Path has taken to date confirms how important and necessary the project is. At the same time, it turns out to be quite an ambitious undertaking to embark publicly upon a path that simultaneously ensures genuine participation, spiritual discernment, theological responsibility, consideration of the specific role of officeholders and attention to the signs of the times—and leads to binding results within a fruitful time frame.

That the Catholic Church in Germany has set out on this experimental path attests to a genuine courage of faith. This places the Church in the perilous position of elucidating, in light of pressing and controversial questions, the gospel's claim to a Church that is contemporary in form, thanks to the "instinctive ability" of the people of God "to discern the new ways that the Lord is revealing to the Church" (Pope Francis). Local Churches in countries with social and ecclesial situations similar to this, as well as the Roman Church leadership, have every reason to be grateful for this courage to face this challenge. After all, the Church must work to shape synodality in different ways, at all times and in every context. In our secular, democratic, and pluralistic society, the demands placed on a synodal Church are unlike those placed on corporative societies in centuries past, and unlike those to which other cultures are subject.

There can be no doubt of the importance for the Synodal Path to issue courageous texts and to launch concrete reforms. But the experience with the process thus selected is of equal importance. For diligent observation and analysis of this process will offer an opportunity to learn the things that help make synodal structures and processes effective and keep them from instead devolving into "talking therapy for the people of the Church" (Claudia Lucking-Michel). I would like to highlight the following from among the factors that in my view will determine the quality of the Synodal Path.

First: bishops, the laity, members of religious orders, the representatives of theology and various associations, councils, and the like will convene in the synodal assemblies on an equal footing, praying, celebrating, and eating together, in such a way as to suspend, as it were, any distinctions of status for the duration of the assemblies.

Second: his creates space for silence, prayer, and listening to the word of Scripture and the workings of the Spirit, in communion and in the depths of the hearts of the faithful.

Third: decision-making processes will seek to strike a balance between the same rights and dignity of all the baptized, on the one hand, and the responsibilities specific to the bishops on the other. These processes will also pay particular heed to the voices of nonmale members of the Synodal Assembly, as there are structural reasons that place these members in a minority.

Fourth: topics will be clearly circumscribed, the process governed by binding rules, meetings conducted in reliable fashion, decisions taken transparently, deliberations conducted in the presence of the media, and, thanks to livestream capability, accessible to all stakeholders.

Fifth: in my view, above and beyond the substantive results generated, the synodality of the Synodal Path will make an important contribution to the learning process to which Pope Francis has called us all through Synod 2021–2023 for the Universal Church and all local Churches. This will set standards for Synodal Paths in the context of liberal democratic societies.

That the Synodal Path sets standards does not, however, mean that the chosen approach could simply be copied in other countries. This can already be seen by looking at the neighboring country of Switzerland. While social conditions, the symptoms of crisis and the calls for reform are largely comparable between the two countries, there are considerable differences in the preconditions involved: the country's multilingual status, combined with the fact that a total of around 30 percent—and in some places even 50 percent—of Church members have a migration background, is hardly conducive to a process in which the elaboration of complex texts plays a central role.

SYNODALITY URGENTLY NEEDS A NEW STYLE

Under Swiss federalism, the approach taken must also take into account the different legal, cultural, and pastoral framework conditions that exist under Swiss national legislation applicable to Church entities. The exercise of pastoral tasks and leadership responsibilities by nonordained theologians has also long been a common practice in the German-speaking areas of Switzerland. The arrangements under national laws that govern Church entities also grant parishes a great deal of autonomy and provide for democratic decisions over the use of Church taxes and in the election of pastors and leadership within the congregations. Some of what the Synodal Path struggles to achieve has already been instituted, at least in part, in German-speaking dioceses in Switzerland.

These specificities, however, and specifically the diversity and already-extant possibilities for the laity to share in responsibility, are arguments not against but rather for the need for synodal processes of communication.

Given the dramatic phenomena of crisis around the loss of social relevance, dwindling human resources and growing distance from the Church, but also given widespread calls for structural reforms, there are many dedicated members of the Church who do not understand that the project announced by the Swiss Bishops' Conference, "Together on the path to renewal of the Church," has led to individual steps but has yet to place the Catholic Church in Switzerland on a synodal path. Not a few read this lack of a structured and institutionally anchored consideration of underlying questions as a sign that Church leadership in this country is missing another opportunity—some have described it as "the last one." They lack the willingness to move past the clerical paradigm, to truly share power and responsibility, and to abandon brittle structures that no longer serve the propagation of the faith and instead constitute an obstacle to discovering the gospel in the first place.

The diocesan phase of Synod 2021–2023 initiated by Pope Francis, which has now been concluded, clearly shows that although faith is still alive among some groups and communities, a very large number of dedicated pastors and Church members scarcely hold hopes that their concerns will be not just heard but taken seriously as well.

As Swiss Catholicism likes to emphasize its diversity along with autonomy that each diocese and each parish enjoys, the temptation to dissociate oneself from the strenuous and necessary conflicts involved in coming up with answers to the crisis is considerable; this retreat can take the form of withdrawing into one's own diocese or one's own pastoral niche, where everything is still right with the world.

This tendency to retreat entails existential risks, however. And these risks impact not just the future of the Church as an institution recognized by society and under public law, but also the effort to discover the relevance of the gospel. The Church can only credibly bear witness to the gospel's message of God's love for the world if it does not dissolve into small communities of faithful unto themselves, but instead bundles its strengths and turns to the world and society in all its complexity, seeking and finding God there (and not in itself alone). Only in this way can it help people both within the Church and beyond achieve a new relationship with the spiritual and existential depth of faith, deriving new hope in difficult times in the process.

THE CHURCH IN SWITZERLAND NEEDS A SYNODAL PATH WORTHY OF THE NAME

If the Catholic Church in Switzerland is to succeed in this "missionary transformation" that Pope Francis tirelessly calls to mind, it needs not just a more synodal style, but also synodal structures and processes that are anchored in the people of God. Synod 2021–2023 opens a window of opportunity to accomplish this. The bishops, together with all those concerned for the future of the gospel and the Church, should seize this opportunity to shape a common Synodal Path that is worthy of the name, taking Swiss circumstances into account and learning from the synodal experiences of neighboring local Churches and the Universal Church.

VENTURE SOMETHING NEW, OR CONTINUE AS BEFORE?

France

Paule Zellitch

Massive upheavals have fundamentally changed the face of the Church in France: just 2 percent of Catholics now take an active part in the life of the Church. The surveys conducted for the World Synod of Bishops revealed that a resurgence of the Church cannot be brought about through the efforts of Church officeholders alone. In addition to bishops who are ready for change, there is a need for empowered Christians who are utterly dedicated to ensuring that "their" Church can become a sign of hope again once more.

TO DESCRIBE THE CLIMATE and the divisions currently emerging among the baptized in France requires briefly taking stock to account for the current features specific to the Church in France. Since the pontificate of Paul VI, several ruptures have occurred in France involving the Church, a very large number of Catholics, and the whole of French society in connection with issues surrounding contraception. These tensions solidified under subsequent pontificates and spread to further areas.

THE CHURCH IS MOBILIZING IN THE FIGHT AGAINST ABUSE

The long pontificate of John Paul II in particular exerted a strong influence on the Church in France, thanks to the support of Cardinal Jean-Marie Lustiger, the archbishop of Paris. Under the banner of "new evangelization," many bishops called for the development of renewal movements, on the one hand, and conservative movements, on the other; both were consistent with the establishment of clericalism. Added to this was a reinterpretation of the Second Vatican Council on the part of universities. From a social and cultural point of view, this affected the types of candidates for the priesthood that emerged from the parishes.

A significant number of church office holders also attempted to influence public debates around issues such as civil marriage for all or the question of surrogate motherhood. Even where they failed to wield this influence, their efforts offered conservative and identitarian fringe groups an opportunity to attract media and political attention. Against this backdrop, the Catholic Conference of the French-speaking Baptized (Conference des Catholique des Baptise.e.s Francophones) was formed in 2009 as an organization that supports the Church and encourages its members to speak up. This conference works with its network to open up and support the efforts of Church institutions and communities to initiate and bring about change.

While the Church tirelessly took up positions on a variety of issues on the basis of natural law, more and more abuses and other crimes came to public attention. The common denominator for all these cases: the silence on the part of bishops and superiors in the religious orders. The discrepancy between word and deed of the official Church, which presented and continues to present itself as an "expert in matters of humanity," led to an immense loss of trust that is ongoing to this day.

In response to pressure from civil society and the possible convocation of a parliamentary commission of inquiry—moves called for by some Catholics who were aware of the impasse into which the French Church had maneuvered itself—the Bishops' Conference of France decided, at the suggestion of Archbishop Georges Pontier, to entrust Jean-Marc Sauve with the task of setting up a commission of inquiry into cases of abuse in the Church. The role of Archbishop Eric de Moulins-Beaufort, president of the Bishops' Conference of France, who joined with other proponents of initiating an investigation, was also decisive in this connection.

The special feature of the Independent Commission on Sexual Abuse in the Catholic Church (CIASE) is that it is not subordinate to the Church hierarchy and includes recognized experts from a variety of disciplines, some of whom are not Catholic. The entire CIASE report was published in October 2021 (cf. Herder Korrespondenz, December 2021, 32–35) and is accessible to all on the relevant website. It contains findings, questions, and numerous recommendations, all stemming from the uncovering of a frightening number of systemic failures throughout our Church.

By and large, the recommendations issued by CIASE exhibit many parallels to the topics addressed by the Synodal Path in Germany. For example, it recommends the creation of independent commissions to introduce an "outsider's" point of view where this may be lacking, thus helping to establish transparent and sustainable procedures and restore confidence.

SOCIETAL STOCKTAKING REVEALS A DRASTIC DOWNTURN IN MEMBERSHIP

The General Assembly of the Bishops in Lourdes in the spring of 2022 showed that the bishops made efforts to take action in light of the results of CIASE, and to address at least some of the issues that often concern questions of leadership. They deployed a variety of working groups and a commission for the support and compensation of people who have been abused by priests. It is chaired by Marie Derain de Vaucresson, an attorney. The Conference of Religious Orders in France (CORREF) also set up a commission for the victims of sexual assault by members of religious orders and elected Antoine Garapon, a prominent member of CIASE, as its chair.

Meanwhile, it remains to be seen how the systemic failures that have been identified will be dealt with in the future. Hearings are set to be held by 2023 and the results made available. The pressing question is this: What is the bishops' roadmap? Will they listen mainly to individuals who are generally favorably disposed to them to begin with?

A glance at French society throws up some frightening figures. Just 36 percent of French people now call themselves Catholics; 2 percent of these are practicing Catholics. Naturally, membership in a parish or Church institution is far from tantamount to agreement with decisions taken by the Church.

All in all, we are faced with a Church in which the majority of Catholics feels abandoned, a Church that has distanced itself from the French people as a result of so many questionable decisions. The persistent downturn in the ranks of the faithful is leading to serious financial problems and, in the more or less near future, to the question of whether the bishops in France still represent the faithful—when they speak to the government, for example.

The Bishops' Conference of France has sent two bishops to *Promesses d'Eglise* (Promises of the Church), an organization of different Catholic movements and associations that have come together in response to the 2018 letter issued by Pope Francis. *Promesses d'Eglise* has opted to proceed on the basis of the "lowest common denominator" in its effort to launch change in society and in the Church.

While this combination of circumstances is quite likely to lead to reforms that are only very modest in nature, we do not want to give up hope: Has not the Holy Spirit, which blows where it will, for many years shown us—sometimes to quite surprising effect—where the dead ends lie?

THE WORLDWIDE SYNODAL PATH SHOWS: THE LAITY MUST BE EMPOWERED

Finally, it should be noted that, in France, there is no Protestant "challenger" of the same relevance as in Germany, that might be in a position to prompt the Catholic Church to evolve further by pointing out other models for ecclesiastical structures. How can we succeed in developing advisory, let alone decision-making, levels that are open to both male and female laypersons? How can the men and women of our day even begin to imagine membership in the Church and the acceptance of what it proclaims as long as Church officeholders fail, by and large, to undertake any truly serious efforts to emerge from their isolation and self-deception?

While France does not have the kind of synodal process seen in the German Synodal Path, we do have some valuable approaches based on the recommendations of CIASE and inspired by processes in other countries, such as Germany or Australia. The worldwide synodal process provides inspiration as well, although it should be pointed out that participation—meaning the dissemination and consideration of the questionnaire from Rome—varies across individual dioceses. Only a few responded directly to this initiative from Rome, which is why the repeated appeals by the pope and the local pressure from a number of laypeople were important to the effort to make headway in this connection.

In some dioceses, the laity were free to participate, and open-minded attitudes were tolerated. But there were also dioceses in which participants were preselected and their contributions subject to review. Although the consultative processes did not chiefly reach those who distanced themselves from parish life (i.e., most Christians in France), as originally envisaged by Pope Francis, they were still useful in that new dynamics emerged where real debates and exchanges occurred.

In the process of disseminating the Roman questionnaire, the Conference of the Baptized launched a campaign to permit every baptized person to respond freely to the questionnaire and thus make effective contributions to the proposals of his or her diocese. In this way, our network directly or indirectly became the driving force for many who were disappointed because their demands were not incorporated into the final document that was conveyed to Rome.

What can be learned from the survey of French Catholics and the countless responses that our network has received? The results show—in keeping with an old reflex on the part of a certain group of the faithful who still assume that they are in the majority—that many French Catholics still rely upon decisions by bishops and other Church officials and expect far too much of them.

One of the key efforts by the Conference of the Baptized is to encourage the laity to play their full role and to become genuine interlocutors who take the initiative and make active contributions to renewal. In short: the point is for the faithful to step out of the condition of passive consumers, and instead, everywhere, to become resources that will effectively promote change.

To achieve this, we need the opportunity to learn from the experiences of others who are already a step or two further than we are. This way, we would certainly benefit from cooperation with German Catholics, who have gradually managed to organize themselves in independent and constructive ways in the effort to make their voices heard. Is the Synodal Path in Germany ready to open itself up to the Conference of the Baptized, and to enter into an exchange with the Catholics of France, who would welcome the interaction?

Another important point, one that has become clear through the survey in the context of the World Synod of Bishops, is a general and rather remarkable substantive overlap with the topics addressed by the Synodal Path in Germany. The future of a Church "for all" rests in the hands of those who have once again become active and brought great energy to the task of reflecting, together, on the need for renewal in Church leadership and doctrine.

In France, however, given the many disappointments already experienced by a very large number of Catholics, there could be serious consequences if these hopes were to be disappointed again. As the mood among the people who took part in the survey suggests, this might be the last great opportunity, an opportunity that the Church's magisterium must seize if it wants to reconnect with its people of faith. At stake is not just the mission of the Church but also, quite pragmatically, its economic survival as well. There is no church tax in France, although the national government does make a contribution in the form of a series of tax exemptions for the various denominations.

THIS MUST NOT REMAIN A DREAM

Spiritual concepts are particularly prominent in the various official documents drawn up in preparation for the Synod, and they can sometimes be found in the contributions of the faithful as well. The aim here is not to contest the importance of spirituality in Christianity. But as the numerous crimes and acts of spiritual abuse have shown us all too well, it is essential not to make spirituality a locus for manipulation.

Moreover, the concept of the dream as underscored in papal pronouncements and magisterial authorities must be placed in perspective, particularly when there are so many very specific areas that require work in the short term and brought to a sound conclusion. Maintaining congruence between word and deed has nothing to do with dreams; this congruence is a solemn ethical requirement, one that no spirituality with a genuinely Christian ambition can circumvent. This is the price of incarnation and hope—in the Christian sense of the term—and it is also the price of resurgence for the Church.

TRUSTING IN THE POTENCY OF THE HOLY SPIRIT

The German Synodal Path from a Nordic point of view

Czesław Kozon

His preparations for the priesthood have brought Czesław Kozon very close to the Church in Germany. Due in part to his personal relationships, its situation is very close to his heart. Yet the German Synodal Path is not easily transferable to the Nordic Church.

THE INVITATION TO SERVE as an observer went out to all the neighboring countries of Germany. From an ecclesiastical point of view, Germany is an important neighbor to Denmark, and to the other Nordic countries as well. The post-Reformation new beginning for Catholic life in most of these countries is owed in large measure to the Catholic Church in Germany. German priests and members of religious orders have dedicated their lives to the Nordic diaspora, and the financial support from Germany, still significant to this day, remains an important prerequisite for many pastoral initiatives.

One reason I am following the German Synodal Path with keen interest is down to the fact that I share the general sense of horror over the numerous cases of sexual abuse. But I am also concerned about how to address this problem. It is absolutely clear—indeed imperative—that sexual abuse in all its forms must be addressed and prevented, and that those who have been affected by it must receive the attention and care they need to heal their wounds.

But the Synodal Path is concerned with more than the topic of abuse. The Synodal Assemblies I attend and in which I actively take part with statements of my own, also address issues that need to be discussed as systemic factors that facilitate abuse. In my view, the discussions of the four Synodal Forums—Power and Separation of Powers in the Church; Priestly Existence Today; Women in Ministries and Offices in the Church; and Living Love in Sexuality and Partnership—pose a challenge to the doctrine and tradition of the Church, because the aim is to make in-depth changes within the institution itself.

This is questionable in and of itself. But in addition to this, there are also topics involved that a local Church cannot pre-emptively decide for itself in isolation to decide for itself. Inasmuch as they are reconcilable with Church doctrine, the content and relevance of the concerns of the Synodal Path must be presented to the Universal Church and discussed at this level.

Naturally, one local Church can always inspire another, but this can only be done within the framework of the common and unchangeable deposit of faith. It is also clear that the topics of the Synodal Path are under discussion in a host of countries, with Catholics also speaking up in favor of changes; this is not always done with the same urgency, however, and often entails different priorities in evangelizing, or a different emphasis, such as family ministry.

In parallel to the Synodal Path in Germany, Catholics around the world—including in the Nordic countries—are involved in the synodal process to which Pope Francis has invited and called us. These two initiatives exhibit similarities as well as major differences. Both processes pursue the objective of making the Church more synodal. This term is often unfamiliar to many of the faithful.

Yet it also documents an attempt to promote community, participation, and mission through listening to one another and, not least, through openness to the inspirations of the Holy Spirit, as part of the effort to make the Church more authentic and hence relevant for all. Whereas the Synodal Path in Germany is focused on the four main topics and the related decision-making processes, Pope Francis has refrained from addressing specific topics and major decisions while at the same time underscoring that this does not involve a democratic and parliamentary process.

While the views and ambitions among Catholics in the North may resemble those of the synodal bodies in Germany, an identical synodal path cannot be superimposed on the Nordic dioceses, nor would it be desirable to do so, given the above-mentioned reasons concerning the priorities involved.

In addition to drawing attention to the fundamental concern for the unity of the Church—which is not an insignificant concern—the course of the Synodal Path now seems to have progressed so far that it is difficult to give the synodal bodies something specific to work with.

There is a great deal of prayer in and around the Synodal Path—prayer to the Holy Spirit in particular. Openness to the Holy Spirit, and faith in what it has done for the Church over the course of centuries, is the best policy.

A PROMISING ADVENTURE FULL OF HOPE

Spain

Luis Manuel Romero Sánchez

A breath of fresh air for the Church of Spain. The national Congress of the Laity, together with its preparatory and follow-up phases, offers lasting hope for the faithful. They expect a new and open-minded Church that will renounce unsustainable structures, overcome clericalism, and heed the needs of laypeople and young people in particular.

ALTHOUGH THE FIRST STAGES of the synodal process in Spain were brief, all in all we experienced a very intense time in which we sensed joy and hope again and again. The most important thing was not the topics we discussed but rather the experience of communion and open, mutual listening among all who belong to the Church (laypeople, members of religious orders, and priests).

In Spain, the process involved essentially all of the dioceses, members of holy orders, Church movements, and lay associations. During our diocesan phase of the synod, the greatest participation and enthusiasm came from the laity, whereas the priests had difficulty becoming engaged in the dynamics.

Yet we experienced an atmosphere of communion and mutual listening. Our encounters were characterized by the desire to "walk together," and to commit ourselves to making our Church less clerical and more synodal.

SPAIN'S LAYPEOPLE AS PROTAGONISTS

In contrast to Germany, the point of departure for our synodal path was not the topic of sexual abuse of minors but rather the National Congress of the Laity, held in Madrid from February 14 to 16, 2020. This Congress of the Laity was meant to serve not as a one-off event but as a synodal process of shared discernment.

During our preparations for this process, in late June 2018, we decided to create a new working style at the Church level, and to work mainly with laypeople; the aim was to create a meeting with synodality and discernment as its hallmark principles. Working groups with lay leadership were formed to organize the congress. The congress itself was understood not as a space for doctrinal lectures but rather as a large, communal gathering.

Attendance at the Congress of the Laity counted more than two thousand people from all the dioceses of Spain; most attendees were laypeople, but members of religious orders, seventy bishops, and numerous priests were also present. During the congress, we dealt with the two main issues of synodality and discernment, as well as four routes the Church must travel: announcement (of the process), support, training processes, and presence in public life.

With so many people sharing their experiences and bearing witness, we were able to draw attention to the richness and plurality of our pilgrim Church in Spain—even though we were naturally also using their statements to uncover its shortcomings.

The main focus of this ecclesial event was upon vocations (baptism), communion (synodality), and mission (living in the heart of the world is part and parcel of the nature of the laity). It was also stressed that the laity are not secondary stakeholders in the Church, but should sense their status as protagonists, alongside pastors, priests and members of the religious orders. We were encouraged to be a people of God who strike out into the world and realize a renewed Pentecost in the lived reality of our particular Churches.

In sum, it can be said that the Congress of the Laity signified the grace of the Holy Spirit for our Spanish Church. It was as if a fresh and new wind were blowing, as one sensed its strong desire to be a Church that goes out into the world, in dialogue with modern-day society.

As this path is to be a sustainable one, during the pandemic we also came up with new formats that would enable us to continue thinking about synodality. In light of the Congress of the Laity, and in spite of the difficulties of contact restrictions, we managed to maintain the joy of our shared path and continue to travel along it, with the aid of the four routes. To this end, a working guide for laypeople was drawn up following the congress.

This is neither a logbook nor a draft of a pastoral plan, nor a users' manual for our parishes; rather, it is a very open-ended document that can serve as a guide to pastoral care throughout our dioceses, associations, and movements. The content opens up new avenues for us while also leaving enough latitude for creativity and freedom in concrete local implementation.

I am convinced that with the Church at this new stage, after some time we will have a common project for the lay apostolate throughout Spain, regardless of the fact that it must be adapted to the respective Church realities and to what is actually possible within each congregation.

In my view, another result of the Congress of the Laity is the constitution of the Advisory Council, which is composed mostly of laypeople. The Council membership includes delegates of the lay apostolate representing the ecclesiastical provinces, associations of laity, ordained persons, and priests. This Council commissions a team whose main missions are to coordinate the work to follow the Congress; to draw up a roadmap or a joint project for all laypeople; and to identify instruments offering support to the delegations of the lay apostolate, the movements, and the associations.

In any event, reference should be made to the working guide issued by the Congress of the Laity. In our view, participation as a layperson in the Synod means continuing to enact in the real world the results of the Congress of the Laity.

CLERICALISM AS THE GREATEST CHALLENGE

When I compare the topics of the Synodal Path in Germany with those of the Congress of the Laity, I am first struck by the different ways in which these topics are arranged and weighted. The main topic of the synodal path in Spain is not sexual abuse, although this is an important topic. Sexualized violence and abuse have also been mentioned in the joint deliberations, and it is undeniable that they have brought about a scandal. They constitute a wound that is very painful to all of us, and to the entire Church.

The myriad topics covered by the Synodal Forums are not at the heart of "our" synodal path, either. In our view the greatest challenge lies in the excessive clericalism that is still very present in Spain. This clericalism keeps laypeople from fulfilling their rightful role in the life of the Church. There are still many steps to be taken in the direction of acceptance and appreciation of the laity, as their vocation is unfortunately still not taken seriously. They are considered to be the remnants of an outdated system and essentially have no decision-making authority. And, while we are discussing the commitment of the laity, of course we must also talk about the role of women in the Church.

The synodal process in Spain formally came to an end on June 11, 2022. This does not mean that we should not continue to practice synodality, however. After all, synodality is a natural form of ecclesial existence and action. The protagonist of this path is the Holy Spirit. That is why it has been important to us, from the outset, to conceive the synodal process as a spiritual path.

We repeatedly placed special emphasis on the dimension of prayer and the celebration of the Eucharist as the culmination and source of synodality. In this, and in concert with Pope Francis, we sought to demonstrate that it is fundamentally important not to stop at formal meetings, but to bring people together to pray together and to celebrate their faith. The preparatory document of the World Synod of Bishops and the *vademecum* provide us with a basic frame of reference. At the same time, we are in constant contact and communion with the General Secretariat of the Synod.

The Church we want to be is one in which we feel needed. The synodal process in Spain helps us recognize the importance of shared responsibility, and thus the need for laypeople to play a leading role. The relationships between bishops and laypeople are very close ones, and yet laypeople do not have shared responsibility with respect to ecclesial structures. Out of a spirit of communion, the synodal path upon which we are embarked also helps us open up new paths for pastoral work. This is because we have found increasing awareness of the parish community.

Ultimately, the pastoral challenge of the synodal process in Spain is to reach the young people and those who "are furthest away from or have turned away from the Church altogether." Moreover, we must continue to work together to overcome clericalism and to achieve participation by the laity in pastoral life, including when there are decisions to be taken.

After all, it is about the desire we all (laypeople, priests, and members of religious orders) have to feel needed in the Church because the Holy Spirit needs us—along the path to a renewed Pentecost. We must be a Church with open doors, a Church that strikes out and accompanies all of humanity, most especially the weakest among us.

TOLERANCE FOR FRUSTRATION EXCEEDED?

Italy

Mauro Castagnaro

We are finally seeing movement in Italy's Church. On several occasions, Pope Francis has asked Italian bishops to embark upon their own synodal path. Many Christians are disappointed and frustrated by the lack of involvement with their reality. Young people in particular find nearly no points of contact with the Catholic Church.

AT ITS 74TH GENERAL Assembly (May 24 to 27, 2021), the Episcopal Conference of Italy (CEI) began the process of creating a synodal path for the Church in Italy. Covering a period of five years, the initiative is divided into three phases (2021–2025). The first phase defines the narrative of listening (2021–2023) in an effort to listen to people at grassroots level. This listening phase will not, however, be confined to the practicing faithful but will also include those who feel that they are at the margins or even outside of the Church. This also includes members of other Churches and religions.

IF NOT FOR POPE FRANCIS, THERE WOULD BE NO SYNODAL PATH IN ITALY

This phase is divided into two stages. The focus from October 2021 to May 2022 will be on the approach to synodality as a form of Church. Running parallel to this will be the consultation process of the World Synod of Bishops entitled "For a synodal Church: Communion, participation, mission."

Then, from June 2022 to May 2023, the exchange is likely to focus on three to four priority themes as defined by the General Assembly of the CEI in May 2022, based on the narratives previously summarized in the local Churches. Building upon this, it will be followed by the "phase of wisdom" (2023–2024). This phase comprises the spiritual interpretation of the reports generated during the two previous years. From them, an attempt will be made to discern, through the *sensus fidei* of the people of God, "what the Spirit says to the Churches."

The third phase, referred to as the "prophetic phase" (2024–2025), will involve preparation of a document of pastoral decisions that will be discussed at the local level. This document will subsequently be presented for adoption by a nationwide assembly and returned to the people of God, who can then anchor its recommendations in the congregations in the subsequent five years (2025–2030).

Following six years of admonition, and at the insistence of Pope Francis, a synodal path in Italy was finally convened. It was also Pope Francis who, at the Fifth Convention of the Italian Church, held in Florence in 2015, called for an attempt to launch, "in a synodal fashion, a deep reflection on *Evangelii Gaudium*." At the General Assembly of the CEI in 2019, he spoke of a "possible Italian Synod." His urgings grew more explicit at the meeting initiated by the Office for Catechesis of the Italian Episcopal Conference in January 2021, where he stated that the Italian Church should embark upon a national synodal process. In April of last year, he approached the Azione Cattolica Italiana (Roman Catholic lay movement) and announced a synodal path that would lead to a Congress in Florence.

FREE DISCUSSION OF THE CHURCH PREVIOUSLY UNHEARD OF

Despite these increasingly urgent calls, the CEI initially cloaked itself in an extended silence. Certainly, this reluctance was down to the fact that free discussion of the Italian Church was still unheard of, as it had always made efforts to present a unified image to the outside world. Critical or simply different voices and experiences were silenced. This trend was reinforced when, from the mid-1980s, a project by "neo-Christians" was prevalent that called for a strong and seamless Catholic identity in an effort to influence society.

While other European Churches convened national synods following the Second Vatican Council to implement and develop the guidelines of the Council locally, Italy opted for the less elaborate and more easily controlled option of holding the national congresses held every ten years (most recently: Teaching the gospel in a changing world [2001–2010] and Education to the good life of the gospel [2010–2020]).

Finally, the Italian bishops then applied the brakes themselves when they witnessed the specter of the Synodal Path of the Church in Germany. This is due to the lack of acceptance by most Italian bishops, who raise issues that are viewed as controversial. In an interview, the president of the CEI, Cardinal Gualtiero Bassetti, observed that the Synodal Path of the German Church had tackled some very particular problems. He believed that the people of Italy would have to cope with fundamental problems that were quite different in nature: loneliness, questions of upbringing, unemployment, and the emotional immaturity driving families apart. The Italian bishops, he continued, would devote themselves to all these problems. But while the celibacy of priests—and, more importantly, the question of priesthood for women—can be presented for discussion, in Bassetti's view these are not the fundamental problems with which the Church and humanity are currently wrestling.

NOW JUST A CHURCH FOR THE SENTIMENTAL AMONG US?

The deeper reason for the cold undertone, however, likely lies in the fact that the bishops see no need for a departure from the past half-century of Church history. After all, this is a period described as a harmonious development, free from twists and turns and conflicts—and not as a Church shaken by the scandals of child abuse by members of the clergy; these are characterized simply as regrettable isolated cases.

But the pandemic has underscored the host of unresolved problems facing a fragile Italian Church and Catholicism, which, as sociologist of religion Franco Garelli observes, "are experiencing an autumn brought on by the process of secularization and the crisis of vocations." Moreover, the internal tensions within Church circles should not be underestimated. There is a growing number of Catholics, known as "cultural" Catholics, who account for up to 45 percent of the total, that continue to distance themselves from religious rites. There is also a steady decline in the ranks of young people who view the model of "Catholicism of the people," conceived in the past, as an anachronism.

A Church with no shortage of fruitful realities and innovative experiences, but that at the same time, by and large, has grown tired, sluggish, and not terribly creative, will obviously fail to make its relevance comprehensible. Over the decades, it has become increasingly alienated from people's lives, as it is still dominated by an ecclesiological model focused on "sacramentalist" pastoral care and on devout and sentimental forms of Christianity. In view of the changes affecting not only civil society but contemporary forms of faith as well, the Church remains stunned and, in spite of myriad charitable initiatives, unable "to say a relevant word" about the serious crises that Italy experienced in 2008 and still experiences to this day.

It is precisely when one seeks to transition from a deductive and application-oriented approach to a method of research and experimentation that builds pastoral action from the bottom up and listens to the voices of the people of God, that the skepticism of an exhausted clergy and the low level of interest on the part of laypeople with little theological training, both with no true confidence in the will to change, will prevail.

As these lines are written, the outcome of the first phase of consultation are still unknown, but there is talk of forty to fifty thousand "synodal groups" that have become active throughout Italy, and of more than 160 diocesan syntheses (from among 220 dioceses) received by the CEI. The impression gained is that this phase has taken shape in patchwork form: with intense commitment in some dioceses, but in many others with a bureaucratic process involving only small groups of "experts."

COMMON ISSUES IN ITALY AND GERMANY

In substantive terms, the final communique of the Permanent Council of the CEI issued on July 9, 2021, pointed out the importance of consulting the grassroots level on questions of meaning and the needs emerging in relation to support for families, young people, the poor and the common good, but also Christian proclamation and initiation, anthropology and the new humanism, the rethinking of structures, and the relationship with public institutions.

In recent months, there has been no shortage of influential voices from grassroots organizations—such as the network of more than thirty associations comprising a large number of groups—who have called for the consideration of organizational issues that are rarely found on the episcopal agenda.

This also includes topics that are at the heart of the German Synodal Path: women's access to ordained offices, the response to and prevention of sexual abuse by members of the clergy, the presence of LGBTQ+ persons, the renewal of the parish organization and the modalities for the Eucharist, the central importance of the word of God, the training of priests, financial transparency and the management of Church assets, the presence of communities of people with migrant backgrounds, the secular character of the state, the commitment to peace and justice and the preservation of creation, ecumenical and interreligious dialogue, and many other topics. But it cannot be said that Italy is home to a mass movement to support structural reforms.

However, the first leaks about the results of the consultation seem to clearly identify the critical points: the image that emerges is one of a Church that is perceived as self-centered, condemning, clerical, rather inattentive to people, and incapable of communicating, particularly with the young people, as it presents itself as moralizing and cultivates an outdated language that is reflected in catechesis and liturgy but fails to offer spirituality.

It is a Church in which laypeople do not matter, women are marginalized, and homosexuals are discriminated against. This shows that the questions that German Catholics are confronting are also a concern to Churches in other countries, Italy included, and that Germany's efforts to communicate the gospel by embarking on new paths are a service that also benefits those living beyond German borders.

AN AWARENESS-RAISING PROCESS TO MEET THE NEEDS OF OUR TIME

Slovakia

Katarina Hulmanová

In Slovakia many people are still drawing on the multilayered experiences of the underground Church. The population, which is still largely shaped by Catholic faith, has shown its readiness for renewal through taking mutual responsibility and working for unity. As a synodal awakening takes place across the world, it is time to draw on the legacy of the former Church network so that synodality becomes the key principle of the Church.

SLOVAKIA, A LITTLE COUNTRY in central Europe with barely five and a half million inhabitants, became the focus of the world's attention in 2021 when Pope Francis made a visit. In that year 60 percent of the population were professing Catholics (including 4 percent from the Greek Catholic Church) and 5.5 percent belonged to the Evangelical Church. The percentage of Roman Catholics dropped from 62 percent in 2011 to 55.8 percent in 2021. And the number of people professing no religion (23.8 percent) or not belonging to any denomination is high: the latter is 6.5 percent. Many factors certainly play a role.

ROOTS IN A DYNAMIC UNDERGROUND CHURCH

In the twenties of the twentieth century religious life boomed, principally because of the development of lay movements and the cooperation between priests and laity, because of Catholic upbringing and the development of the Caritas organization. This development was interrupted by the Second World War, the period of the Slovak State and the communist revolution in 1948. The trauma of the Slovak state and the war has marked the development process to this day. Also, we have only half-heartedly come to terms with the crimes of communism.

This period of communist rule was the time when the lay apostolate began. This is associated with the name of the Croatian priest Tomislav Kolakovic. The priest, who came to Slovakia in 1943, founded small communities to support the Slovakian and Czech Church. He did this principally by introducing them to streams of Catholic thinking that would only bear fruit much later at the Second Vatican Council. This thinking related to the understanding of the Church as the mystical Body of Christ, the people of God, the renewal of the liturgy, a stronger participation by the laity in the life of the Church, collegiality, and ecumenism.

In reality, Kolakovič prepared our Church for the time of persecution. In the fifties, members of his community went to jail. However, after their return in the sixties they continued to implement his legacy. The best known of them, Vladimir Jukl and Silvester Krčmery, founded Bible study and prayer groups in schools and universities. The establishment of this underground Church network took place in lively cooperation with courageous priests and members of holy orders who lived the spirit of service and unity.

THE PANDEMIC AS A TRIGGER OF CRITICAL AND CREATIVE PROCESSES

The COVID-19 pandemic is hitting Slovakia hard. It is noticeable that the regulations that were introduced to limit the gathering of believers were disproportionately harsh compared to those relating to nonreligious gathering and also in comparison to neighboring states. People are feeling uncomfortable about this dissonance.

Vaccination has split believers. It is important to know that in Slovakia we are very inclined to believe false information. Black-and-white thinking, unhealthy forms of nationalism in connection with hate, along with distrust of foreigners and minorities are unfortunately still widespread.

Yet the pandemic has also made us creative: new forms of pastoral care have been established, individual pastoral care has been strengthened, and the virtual world has brought new possibilities for creativity. As part of the regulations, communion in the hand has been introduced, which produced a certain amount of upset among both laity and priests, because communion on the tongue is still seen among us at the right way to receive it.

TRIPLE BOOSTER, PAPAL VISIT, WAR IN UKRAINE, COMMUNITY ETHOS

One thing has shaped us even more than the supposed alienation from liturgical practices: the visit of Pope Francis in 2021, which has had a lasting effect on Slovakia. The pope showed us the people on the edge of society and of the Church. Even if no significant or concrete results can so far be drawn from this, it has shown us where the pastoral priorities should lie. We hope that as people consider his speeches about the synodal path something of the new spirit that he has brought to us will be reflected.

Our country is currently shaken by the war in Ukraine. It affects Slovakia in a very real way. The Church, and in particular Caritas, but also lay movements, religious orders, and many families are right on the front line in giving help. One of the best qualities of Slovaks has shown itself—their strong sense of solidarity and willingness to volunteer. Even though it is happening on a different level, the commitment to fellow human beings is also reflected in the synodal process.

The synodal process in which Slovakian believers are taking part is an integral part of the worldwide synodal process. We see this synodal awakening as an opportunity to introduce new ways of living together, especially in parishes. The process is therefore taking place primarily at parish level, where people meet in small groups so that everyone can be heard. We hope that this will give more and more believers the courage to take responsibility for the Church and society.

For us, participation at all levels is a completely new experience: laypeople really have responsibility for the process and have a voice. Everyone is listened to. The experience of Church as community in the sense of the Second Vatican Council is thereby noticeably deepened. The meetings bring out terrific new ideas.

We see the synodal path, as the pope has initiated it, as a cultivation of ourselves, our community, and our relationships. It is neither to do with the creation of new structures (although the whole process is very well structured and organized) nor about the sharing of "power," nor about external "success." Every person has their own pace and their own capabilities for getting involved. Those should be the key concerns. Several synodal groups are also trying to reach people who find themselves on the edge of Church life.

The theme of women in the Church is not being discussed in a confrontational way, and the ordination of women, as it has been debated in Germany, is not under discussion here. It is not being artificially suppressed as you might think; rather, there is simply no interest in this theme, not even from the women themselves. This possibly comes from the fact that women are as little represented in decision-making positions in the Church as they are in Slovakian society generally, whether in politics or business. That does not completely exclude the theme from the agenda, but we simply have a different focus.

One of the less discussed themes is also the question of gender equality. Discussions are also taking place with so-called rainbow Christians, even in communities that present themselves as ultraconservative. However, it is not about forcing a consensus, which because of the diversity of opinion would not be viable, but about giving equal rights to everyone: taking people seriously and at least listening to what they have to say.

We are convinced that listening in a spirit of respect and valuing people is bound to succeed. The goal of the synodal process is discernment, while being true to the word of God and the teaching of the Church, with sensitivity toward the voice of the people of God. Otherwise, the synodal process could easily fall victim to ideological interests and political battles.

In this respect, international exchange and cooperation, following the example of the European Laity Forum, could help us to gain new perspectives. We believe that dialogue is meaningful and would like to take it deeper.

THE PATH EMERGES WHILE WALKING

Ireland

Nicola Brady

It is still uncertain what exactly the Synodal Pathway in Ireland will look like. The starting signal has been given, and the goal is clear: to hold a National Synodal Assembly in five years. Enough time to practice a new synodal togetherness. This is indispensable, as I show by the rapid secularization in what was once the "most Catholic country in the world." In view of the synodal process so far, however, there is hope that a large number of the faithful are willing to give the Church another chance.

ON MARCH 10, 2021, the Irish Catholic Bishops' Conference announced a new Synodal Pathway for the Catholic Church in Ireland, leading to the holding of a National Synodal Assembly within the next five years. The guiding question for this Irish Synodal Pathway is this: What does God want from the Church in Ireland at this time? In advance of the public announcement, in early March the members of the Irish Bishops' Conference met with Cardinal Mario Grech and Natalie Becquart of the General Secretariat for the Synod of Bishops to discuss the ways in which synodality could enrich the Irish Church, and how Ireland could contribute to global efforts to embed synodality across the Universal Church.

ABOUT THE PROCESS

The first two-year phase of Ireland's synodal journey is to be an open-minded time of "listening and discernment" and will aid in preparation for the subsequent formal, synodal process. To take this work forward, in June 2021 the Bishops' Conference announced the establishment of a Steering Committee comprising episcopal and lay members with a range of different backgrounds and fields of expertise.

The Steering Committee, which the Bishops' Conference selected me to chair, is supported by a Task Group that has established a network of delegates from dioceses and other organizations that wish to participate in the synodal process. Each of Ireland's twenty-six dioceses has appointed an ordained or lay delegate to this network. The Task Group will keep delegates apprised of the development of the synodal process, offer training opportunities in areas such as presentation skills and networking, and open up a space in which delegates can get to know each other and provide peer support.

The aim of the preparatory phase of exchange at the local and national levels is to identify the methodology best suited to exploring God's will for the future shape of the Church in Ireland. The Steering Committee will produce a report with the findings obtained and make recommendations on the trajectory of the Synodal Pathway going forward. During the subsequent, second phase, which is anticipated to last for approximately three years, the Bishops' Conference will attempt to implement the recommendations and structures that involving the faithful and conducting the Synodal Assembly or Assemblies will require.

In their March 2021 announcement of the Synodal Pathway, the Irish bishops made it clear why the Church in Ireland needs the synodal process. They pointed to the leading role of the pope, his apostolic exhortation *Evangelii Gaudium* and the encyclicals *Laudato Si'* and *Fratelli Tutti.* In addition to the pontifical call to reach out to the peripheries in a spirit of solidarity, the bishops recalled in particular the pope's message to the people of Ireland during his 2018 visit to Dublin for the World Meeting of Families, in which he spoke of the promise of a new Pentecost and called the Irish people to open their hearts to the work of the Holy Spirit.

In addition to referencing the teachings of Pope Francis, the bishops went on to name some of the specific features of the Irish context, such as the profound secularization of our country. Ireland has undergone a rapid social transformation over the past fifty years that has led to a major decline in the practice of faith and in the number of vocations to the priesthood and the religious life.

As with other national synodal pathways, the situation in Ireland has been profoundly shaped by shocking revelations of abuse surrounding the Church. Successive investigations and inquiries into this abuse have further reminded us of the deep trauma felt by so many within the Church and the need for inner healing and hope: these include the report into the diocese of Ferns (2005), the Murphy report into the archdiocese of Dublin (2009), the Ryan report on the abuse of children in institutions (2009), the report on the diocese of Cloyne (2011), the McAleese inquiry into Magdalene laundries (2013) and the inquiry into mother and baby homes (2021). Arising from the painful legacy of this abuse crisis, there is a cry for transparency and accountability in Church governance.

Conscious of historical context on the island of Ireland, the bishops also emphasized the need to promote peacemaking one hundred years on from the partition of Ireland. At the same time, they recognized how much Ireland's population has changed since then, pointing to the need for a culture of welcome and integration for migrants and the many newcomers living on the island.

LINK WITH THE WORLD SYNOD

The role of the family as "domestic Church" had really come to the fore in response to the restrictions imposed due to the COVID-19 pandemic, and bishops hoped that the synodal pathway could help support family participation in the life of the Church. A related concern was the need to enlist the energy and gifts of our young people, forming and enabling them to be missionaries to each other and inviting them to spread the good news not only in Ireland but around the world.

As an additional decisive topic, the bishops identified a need for greater acknowledgement of the high level of commitment on the part of many women in the Irish Church. They underscored a need to hear women's deep concerns and formally recognize their role. This calls for new models of coresponsibility and leadership involving all laypeople—women and men, including those who feel ignored, excluded or forgotten.

This first two-year phase of Ireland's national Synodal Pathway coincides with the Synod on Synodality announced by Pope Francis for the Universal Church (2021–2023). The Steering Committee in Ireland has decided to integrate the work of both processes so that each can support and inform the other.

The Committee is currently working collaboratively with dioceses and a wide range of other groups and organizations to encourage people to engage with the work being undertaken for the Universal Synod, recognizing that this offers a helpful opportunity to assess where we are in relation to the understanding and practice of synodality as we set out on our own national journey. The reflections on this experience of listening and exchange will provide insights into the Church—past, present, future—from which we can learn how best to continue the synodal journey at the national level.

At the time of writing, we as the Steering Committee are currently working to prepare a National Pre-synodal Assembly that will convene this network of delegates from the dioceses with bishops for a day of dialogue and discernment before the final report of the Catholic Church of Ireland is submitted to the Vatican within the framework of the Universal Synodal Path.

At this early stage there is great variety in the approaches and methodologies employed in parishes and dioceses. Despite this, one of the early benefits of this synodal journey is that new relationships are developing across diocesan boundaries, helping the Church to be more integrated as a whole and facilitating the sharing of ideas and resources.

PROPONENTS AND OPPONENTS

As reports from dioceses and other organizations have not yet been received, it is too early in the process to offer any conclusions based on the experience of dialogue to date. But the work of the Steering Committee does permit some interesting observations through its work to date, particularly as concerns the shared notion of synodality.

As the invitation issued at the outset went out to *all* the baptized to become involved on behalf of the Synodal Pathway and help shape a vision for the future of the Church, the process in Ireland remains the effort of persons of very disparate backgrounds. Particularly at the outset, the language of synodality posed a challenge from a communications perspective, with many people unfamiliar with the concept. Some viewed the term itself as the domain of the Church hierarchy and not relevant to them.

At the same time, there have been and are many who recognize synodality as a great opportunity for the Church and are pleased to respond to the invitation to take part in the process. Thanks to the considerable efforts made, awareness of the term, its etymology, and its special significance in a Catholic Church context is growing steadily. Language such as that of a "listening Church" and "journeying together" is making the concept more accessible to the faithful. There remains nevertheless a great deal of work to do before people can gain a real understanding of synodality as spiritual practice.

Along with the clear proponents of the Synodal Pathway, some individuals and groups are also reluctant to participate in, or are proactively opposed to, this work, for fear that it will lead to further fracturing of an already weakened Church at a time when we already need to rebuild in the wake of the COVID-19 pandemic.

The pandemic posed a hurdle not just in terms of the methodical execution of the Synodal Pathway—although digital networking also helped drive developments that promote the process (such as intensification of international exchange). The effort to involve the faithful in the synodal process also called for great sensitivity to the traumatic impact of the pandemic in terms of bereavement, isolation, and financial pressures. Some dioceses chose to ask specific questions about the pandemic experience as part of their synodal process, demonstrating that a focus on synodality is already helping us to become more responsive pastorally as a Church.

We have seen much in this synodal process to date that has given us great hope and encouragement. On balance, notwithstanding the very vocal opposition of those who were opposed to synodality, from the outset there has been significant goodwill toward Ireland's Synodal Pathway. If this goodwill is to contribute to the rebuilding of trust in the Church, it will require a long-term commitment and a demonstration that the contributions people make will be honored.

For the Synodal Pathway to have the potential to lead to lasting changes in the form of the Church, we will need to reflect in a self-critical way on the extent to which we have been able to reach out to the margins of our Church communities and engage in honest dialogue with people about the barriers to belonging in the Church. We need to be prepared to address the fact that we have made mistakes and will continue to make mistakes as we journey along our Synodal Pathway, and be open to learning as we journey together. This will include learning from our brothers and sisters in other parts of the world about how synodality is practiced and experienced in different contexts.

REAL LIFE IS WHERE TO FIND THE SIGNS OF THE TIMES

United States

Rene Reid

Catholic Christianity in the United States is divided. Many people feel that the bishops are out of touch with real life. Young people especially feel that they are not understood and are leaving the Church. At the same time, there is a high level of commitment on the part of laypeople, who have not given up hope and are fighting to have their questions heard. In substance these issues are very close to those under discussion in the context of the Synodal Path in Germany.

EVER SINCE THE SECOND Vatican Council, one in three Catholics in the United States of America has left the Church. One of the reasons for this is that the U.S. hierarchy's attitude is felt by many to be problematic, being by and large more insistent on maintaining and enforcing the old Church rules than demonstrating compassion for human beings and their real-life problems.

THE WORLDWIDE SYNODAL PROCESS IS MAKING SLOW PROGRESS

The way in which holders of ecclesiastical office handle topics like abortion, reproductive rights, divorce and remarriage, plus decisions on who is allowed to receive holy communion, is driving more and more Catholics of all sexes away from the Church. Once young people reach adulthood and find these rules incomprehensible, as well as being outraged at the Church's treatment of women and homosexuals, they leave in droves. Revelations of sexual abuse scandal in the clergy has triggered yet another wave of leavers.

The mood of a large proportion of the faithful in the United States of America is also reflected in how they relate to the bishops. In a nutshell, the situation between bishops and laypeople is, with few exceptions, a major issue. Too many of our bishops are more concerned with refusing the Eucharist to our President Joe Biden and the former Speaker of the House of Representatives Nancy Pelosi because of their pro-choice attitude than with organizing diocesan synods.

One example is the letter from conservative bishops to the German bishops, in which they declare that the latter's Synodal Path is undermining the credibility of Church authority. Well over half of the signatories come from the United States. Even if this accounts for only a small percentage of all 274 U.S. American bishops, they are extremely vociferous in expressing their displeasure and are obviously very worried about the Synodal Process in Germany.

Despite the resistance of the conservative U.S. bishops to setting Pope Francis's synodal process in motion, many local parish congregations offer an opportunity for synodal discussion right after Mass. The problem is that there are often limitations with regard to the issues that can be addressed, which means that not all topics can be discussed openly. Furthermore, if the number of participants is too great, genuine debate cannot develop. This is different in the “Small Christian Communities,” of which there are plenty in the United States. Many of the small synodal assemblies send their reports directly to the Synod Office in Rome because they are afraid that their thinking might be filtered or called into question by the bishops.

YEARNING FOR RENEWAL OF SEXUAL MORALITY

What are the preoccupations of Catholics in the United States? First, social concerns focused on the relationship between Church and society that make people insist on more emphasis on the social dimension of the gospel, both in the Church and in civil society. This includes demands such as greater consideration for people living in poverty, equality for women, or ending the dismissive treatment of Catholics who, for various reasons, do not or cannot live according to Church doctrine.

This focuses both on people who are part of the LGBTQ community and remarried divorcees. Many Catholics wish they might be accepted into full communion with God’s children and granted access to the sacraments. In particular, they want the invitation to the Eucharist to address all people and be understood as nourishment for those who need it, rather than a reward for those who are perfect. The Eucharist should express the unity of all God’s children in their diversity of faith and practice of religion, not act as an instrument of dogmatic austerity and marginalization.

Connected to the desire for acknowledgement of all human individuals, irrespective of their particular sexuality, is the hope that the Catholic Church might develop a fundamentally new view of sexuality. The sexual morality of *Humanae Vitae* is rejected by an overwhelming majority—92 percent of Catholic women in the United States—

and young people especially long for ethics that emphasize the loving side and spiritual aspects of sexuality.

When it comes to abortion, the Church should be concerned not only for the unborn child but for all children born into this world. Those children living in dire poverty are especially in need of care throughout their lives. This requires consistency in the ethics of life, consistency that makes the Church support politicians much more strongly in matters of poverty. Moreover, the Church bears responsibility in the struggle against racism and the debate on the subject of immigration.

EXTENSION OF THE RIGHT OF ALL BAPTIZED ADULTS TO THEIR SAY

In addition to social matters, the American faithful are concerned about issues centering on Church structures. One central issue is that leadership structures should reflect synodality. Proposals have been mooted to extend the right of all the baptized to participate both in pastoral matters and decisions on morality or questions of faith. Furthermore, the Church itself could become more synodal if qualified laypeople—irrespective of sex or family status—were involved in leadership of the congregation and could take charge of services or even conduct prayers. One possible way would be, for instance, to deploy parish councils as leadership bodies in the parishes.

There are many reform groups in the United States actively committed to renewal of the Catholic Church, especially with regard to the involvement of women in all aspects of ecclesiastical life. Among them are, for example, Future Church or Call to Action. Although their objectives have a different focus, they are all united in their desire for the Church to become more inclusive and synodal.

If the Church wants to have a future, it must learn to acknowledge and value the "richness and diversity of gifts and charisms" of its members, including the lowliest among them. It must get used to diversity of opinions and respond to the invitation from the Holy Spirit to become a Church more strongly oriented to community among brothers and sisters with equal rights as disciples.

Achieving this will not only demand the opening of all Church offices to those currently excluded even though they are qualified (women, married men, LGBTQ people, etc.), but also the revision of leadership structures as mentioned earlier. Opening up the offices would not be sufficient on its own for a fundamental renewal of the Church's countenance. A new understanding of priesthood needs to be developed. If laypeople and clergy are to work together as equal partners, this must also be reflected at decision-making level, power sharing being a keyword here.

Giving a say to the baptized members in the selection (and retention) of their leaders, including parish priests and bishops, would be part of the synodal way of cooperation. In particular, the decision as to who presides over the eucharistic liturgy should be made by the entire community of the baptized.

Setting up systems of accountability could contribute little by little to overcoming the authoritarian character of clericalism. It is important, too, to improve the training of candidates for the priesthood by no longer keeping seminarians isolated from the rest of society. The power of existing clerical structures often results in priests and bishops being formed in such a way that they keep their distance from other people and do not possess the leadership qualities they need to cope with the tasks that come with their priestly authority.

WILLINGNESS TO DEVELOP IS INDISPENSABLE

Regular talks between members of the Catholic Church Reform International network are a constant reminder that the preoccupations of many of the faithful in the United States are also issues in other parts of the universal Church. In our synodal meetings, we seek quietness in prayer and invoke the Holy Spirit to guide us during our intensive reflection on each of the matters we address.

We are currently about to organize a worldwide online synod with seventeen participating countries: Australia, Brazil, France, India, Ireland, Italy, Japan, Kenya, Mexico, the Netherlands, New Zealand, Pakistan, the Philippines, South Africa, Spain, the United Kingdom, and the United States The first two meetings have already shown that there is a consensus to the effect that we must make our currently monarchical Church into a synodal community like that of the early Church, in which the people of God participate fully, and women are involved in an equal capacity at all levels of service. Without these two transformations, our Church will not be able to survive in the world of today. We acknowledge that all the Church's teachings are linked to their time and culture, that they are transitory and can change, that they need to be updated or further developed in the light of contemporary scriptural research and theology. Furthermore, the Church must be prepared, as an institution led by human beings, to admit to its fallibilities, to be humble and allow itself to be changed. It is a living institution that ought to be dynamic, not static.

All this requires not only reinforcement of the way documents from the Second Vatican Council are received and implemented, but also, above and beyond that, the convocation of a third Vatican Council. Our present life deserves an appropriate debate with the "signs of the times," as well as the integration of handed-down traditions, as God ever gifts and reveals himself anew.

TRAVELING COMPANIONS AND WITNESSES ALONG THE SYNODAL PATHWAY

From a French point of view

Didier Berthet and Jérôme Vignon

Shaping the future together: when it comes to synodal questions and answers, the Church in Germany is a role model. We become witnesses to ensuring different points of view. This is where the actual character of synodality comes into play. This entails not just a fair and suitable process in the democratic sense of the term, but also an attitude of mutual acceptance and faith in the abilities of the synthesis offered by the *sensus fidei* of the Assembly.

IN OUR ROLE AS French observers, ever since the first Synodal Assembly of the Synodal Path in Frankfurt, we have felt like traveling companions to our Catholic brothers and sisters in Germany. As bishop of the diocese of Saint-Die in the Vosges, and as a layman engaged in the movements of social Christianity, together we are a precise representation of the parity of clergy and laypersons that also determines the composition of the German Synodal Path.

THE FRUITFULNESS OF DISAGREEMENT

Our experience of the three-day Synodal Assembly is particularly intense when differences of opinion emerge or emotional statements are made. That is when we live our mission as observers to the fullest. We become witnesses to ensuring different points of view. This is where the actual character of synodality comes into play. This entails not just a fair and suitable process in the democratic sense of the term, but also an attitude of mutual acceptance and faith in the abilities of the synthesis offered by the *sensus fidei* of the Assembly, in the sense understood by Pope Francis.

We are also witnesses in view of the communities of French Catholics that have commissioned us to report back on what we have experienced. The October 2021 report on the sexual abuse of young people and vulnerable persons by clergy in France led to an admission of responsibility and a process of structural reforms in our Church that was modeled after the Synodal Path in Germany. That is why it is important to share the German approach—from a methodological point of view and, most importantly, from the point of view of what this approach says about the faith of German Catholics.

PRIMACY OF PRAYER AND LITURGICAL CELEBRATION

This includes the primacy of prayer and liturgical celebration, the central focus on the experiences of the victims, the virtue of calm listening, the vast importance of the common priesthood of the baptized, and, not least, the awareness of a German responsibility toward the Universal Church. Our reports are meeting with growing interest; they give rise to great hopes for change by some and are viewed with concern by others. Where reforms are concerned, the French

Church itself is divided, as both the state of our society and the recognition of our faults must be taken into account.

Drawing on our experiences, our German friends have repeatedly asked for our views on the Synodal Path. We can well understand that the credibility that must be restored following the sexual abuse scandal is one of the main motivations for the path taken. For if the Church causes a scandal, it cannot fulfill its mission in a coherent or fruitful way. Yet this credibility is not confined to meeting the presumed expectations of civil society. Rather, it obliges us to strive for even greater fidelity to Christ and the gospel, for they alone are credible.

At the ecclesiological level, the Trinity at the origin of the Church must also be remembered, the Church is at the same time the people of God (i.e., synodal), the Body of Christ (i.e., hierarchical) and the temple of the Holy Spirit (i.e., charismatic). This third dimension, the dimension of the Holy Spirit and of charismata, offers us an opportunity to catch our breath, a kind of suspension we can use to broaden our view of the ever-recurring and at times very narrow question of the power to be exercised in the Church.

This is how the Holy Spirit helps us transcend an unduly functional grasp of the Church, incorporating a more symbolic, sacramental, and vital dimension in the process. It should also always be borne in mind that the Synodal Path is not about the German Church but about the Church in Germany. This is a very important consideration, as it will make it possible to receive the fruits of this important path with even greater calm and depth.

Ultimately, it is striking to note that a shared sensitivity and broad consensus have since emerged among the stakeholders of the Synodal Path. Still, the path has yet to come to an end. In light of this, in our view greater efforts ought to be made in the Synodal Assemblies to ensure that all opinions are heard with the same respect and the same attention. Any pronouncements in the style of a collective judgement should be avoided in an effort to strengthen the sense of cohesion.

As the gospel teaches us, the Holy Spirit breathes where it wishes; if we really want to listen to the Holy Spirit, we must always grant it this freedom!

SYNODALITY UNFOLDED ANEW

Argentina

Carolina Bacher Martínez

One topic seems to preoccupy the whole world more than any other: the question of participation by laypeople, especially women, in the Church. A central focus of the synodal process in Argentina is esteem for women, who suffer from inequality and injustice throughout Latin America.

PROVINCIAL COUNCILS AND diocesan synods have been part of the Latin American Church ever since its earliest days. The synodal momentum was reinforced with the founding of the Episcopal Council of Latin America (CELAM), the body that promotes the General Conferences of the Latin American and Caribbean Episcopate, in the wake of the Second Vatican Council. CELAM recently organized new forms of involvement and shared reflection, the fruits of which were incorporated into the first Latin American Ecclesiastical Assembly in November 2021.

In faithfulness to its pastoral tradition, the Ecclesiastical Assembly formulated twelve pastoral challenges, which can be paired under the terms "Church—World." Those that were formulated exclusively for the Church community are listed first.

KEY TOPICS FOR THE CONTINENTAL CHURCH ASSEMBLY

The challenges consist in renewing the notion and experience of the Church as the people of God in community with the richness of its service in the light of the word of God and the Second Vatican Council, while avoiding clericalism and favoring pastoral conversion. They also include promoting the formation of synodal structures and enabling active participation of women in ecclesiastical office, leadership, and decision-making.

Also at the ecclesiastical assembly, set topics were chosen to express social challenges. These include, in particular, hearing the cry of the poor, marginalized, and excluded; promoting and defending the dignity of life and the human person from conception to natural death; and supporting indigenous peoples and people of African descent in the defense of their lives, lands, and cultures.

The third group of topics comprises those challenges that connect the pastoral with the social axis: first, to acknowledge and value the role of young people as protagonists of change in society and the Church; second, to support victims of social and ecclesiastical injustices in processes of recognition and reparation; third, to promote and involve laypeople in matters of cultural, political, social, and ecclesiastical change; fourth, to reaffirm and prioritize integral ecology in parish congregations and reform training programs and seminars by addressing the relevant subjects: indigenous peoples, inculturation, and interculturalism, a new social way of thinking in the Church.

The Church in Argentina cannot keep itself apart from this post–Vatican Council regional process. Of the nearly seventy dioceses and other Church institutions in the country, several already have experience with a synod or diocesan assembly. For others, however, it is a new experience. Pope Francis's call to deepen synodality has motivated the organization of several diocesan synods. In some cases, the processes initiated at local level, participatory processes as proposed by the Latin American Church Assembly, and preparation for the synods from 2021 to 2023 were partially implemented, while the work was done successively in other cases.

Aiming to improve participation, the Conference of Argentine Bishops (CEA) appointed episcopal project leaders for nationwide motivation work, who in turn formed bigger pastoral teams that invited diocesan delegates to virtual prayer, information, reflection, and group work meetings in the pastoral regions and encouraged creativity in diocesan organization and listening processes. After various consultations and estimates, the diocesan teams worked on the elaboration of the local report, which was sent by May 31, 2022, to an editorial team working with the bishops, who are responsible for synthesizing them into a national report.

Although the finished report had not been received before we went to press, some informal conversations indicate that the issue of abuse will play a part in the consultations, though not necessarily a prominent one. Nevertheless, it should not be forgotten that the CEA has already set up a pastoral council for the protection of minors and vulnerable adults, made up of clergy, religious, and laypeople as an advisory body to the Conference of Bishops and the various dioceses on safeguarding against abuse of conscience and power as well as sexual abuse.

With regard to the issue of women's participation in the Church and society, three pointers give an outline of the most recent synodal processes.

WOMEN SHOULD SHOW A QUALIFIED PRESENCE IN MANAGEMENT POSITIONS

The archdiocese of Cordoba is the local Church in Argentina with the longest history of diocesan synods. In October 2015, Archbishop Carlos Jose Nanez convened the twenty-first diocesan synod with the theme of First Proclamation of the Gospel in the presence of the diocese. The consultations took place in congregational assemblies, which complemented the diagnosis, and were accompanied by an editorial team that prepared the working document.

The synod took place from September to October 2018 and was completed with a closing document containing the fruits of the synodal process condensed into five points from the discussions: holiness as a horizon, synodality as the key to identity, joyful and contemporary proclamation, respectful handling of the good news, and a poor Church living the option for the poorest of the poor and the suffering.

Another key issue in the synod is the subject of women. Women's participation in all pastoral areas is to be honored and encouraged. This includes a qualified female presence in decision-making areas connected to pastoral care in the archdiocese and parishes, and also in the formation of future priests.

As part of a poor Church with a commitment to the poorest and suffering, it was decided that the care of women in difficult and critical situations of abuse and violence should be in services of "listening and assistance," both in the parish congregation and locally.

A further example is the first synod of the archdiocese of Buenos Aires, which took place between August and November 2021. After the convocation of the synod by Mario A. Poli in 2017, a synodal team was set up to design the various phases of consultation and drive forward discernment at regional level. Next, a synodal reflection team was assembled to systematize the results of deliberations and prepare an interim document that was presented to the congregations for reflection and comment. After this last process, the final working document was drafted for use in reflection by the assembly of synods.

The result of this assembly was the document "Walking Together in Spirit to Renew the Mission in Buenos Aires."

In it, Mary's visitation to Elizabeth and the Magnificat are received as biblical icons. Thus, the closing document states that Mary and Elizabeth are two female protagonists in history who embody the dignity of women and the fulfillment of their mission. They express the place Jesus gave to women. Together with his mother, it was the women who went with him to the very end. Accordingly, the paragraph ends with the words, "A Church that is all too fearful may be on the defensive, mistrust discourse about women's rights and only point out possible errors in these assertions."

The document includes women in the proposals for cooperation and sees them in the context of the socially wounded. The text explicitly advocates acknowledgement of their dignity and esteem for their contribution to society and in the Church. Furthermore, it recommends that thought be given to the possibility of priesthood for women.

It should be mentioned in this context that the Women's Section of the CEA Department of Lay Affairs (DEPLAI) in cooperation with the Latin American Church Assembly has established an online forum on the subject of women. The initiators organized a survey to hear the views of people associated in any way with DEPLAI in Argentina, mainly but not only women, from which input to the consultation processes was created in the run-up to the assembly.

These brief examples show that the treatment of women's issues in Argentina takes into account the feminization of poverty and other problems, valuing their contribution to society and the Church, and the necessity to offer qualified spaces for involvement in Church affairs, and puts them at the forefront of attention.

Looking back in conclusion, the synodal processes initiated in the Church in Argentina admits two local challenges for consultation and participation: one is the need for technical discussion about the elaboration and execution of the consultations. This would make it easier to capture the views of the people of God and other interlocutors in the country in a more comprehensive and controlled manner and take into consideration the appropriate means of communication for the inclusion of contributions from ordinary people.

On the other hand, it is advisable to optimize linkages of global, regional, and national processes in order to avoid overlaps between consultation and participation bodies, which might jeopardize the implementation of certain agreements already reached and, in some cases, noted as binding at diocesan level.

TRADITION TURNS INTO AN ANSWER

Chile

Catalina Cerda-Planas and Pascale Larré

When news of the abuse scandal in Chile went public, twenty-nine of the thirty-one bishops in office at the time offered their resignation to the pope. The Church's loss of credibility and the pent-up frustration of the faithful also precipitated into the numbers leaving the Church. Even before the worldwide synodal process began, the Church in Chile had already developed synodal elements.

AN INTENSIVE AND comprehensive synodal process has been going on in Chile in recent years. It started before 2021, when Pope Francis announced that the theme of the 2023 General Assembly of bishops in Rome would be synodality in the Church. Latin America has a strong tradition of synodality. Given this fact, the most recent dialogue processes in Chile can be declared as part of this tradition. The loss of trust in the Chilean Church, the ongoing decline in numbers of the faithful, and the effects on public and private lives of the grave crisis caused by abuse within the Church have nonetheless given rise to new processes of listening and communal spiritual discernment.

NO CONFIDENCE IN THE CATHOLIC CHURCH ANY LONGER?

Only 36 percent of the Chilean population say that they have confidence in the Church. That is the lowest number of all the countries in the entire continent (cited from *Corporación Latinobarómetro* 2018). The decline in the number of Catholics in the past two decades is alarming for Chile: whereas 70 percent of the population described themselves as Catholic in 2006, the number in 2019 was only 45 percent. Interestingly, this trend was already beginning to appear even before the abuse scandal in the Chilean Church started to grow in the public's consciousness in 2010.

Renunciation of Catholicism on this scale does not mean that association with other (evangelical) Christian Churches has increased proportionately. The number of people describing themselves as evangelical shows only a small increase in the past fifteen years (from 14 to 18 percent). National survey data show the strongest growth in the group stating "no religion" (12 to 32 percent). However, only a few describe themselves as atheists, as there are various other faiths represented in the Chilean population.

The key to the frustration among the faithful, especially those leaving the Church, seems not to be the serious and reprehensible abuse cases themselves, but the Church's handling of the subject, notably and above all the indifference or even cover-up of abuse cases and the systemic issues that lie behind the crisis. These include "unhealthy" everyday relationships between male and female Catholics, the dearth of opportunities for participation by the faithful, clericalism, coclericalism of laypeople, and the lack of sensitivity toward the religiosity and daily problems of the faithful. This has led to deep disappointment, disenchantment, and frustration, and thus to a substantial weakening of Christian community life.

FOR A PROPHETIC CHURCH

In light of this scenario and the urgent need of decisions for genuine conversion of the Church, pastoral project leaders, vicars, and bishops were invited to a spiritual discernment meeting in June 2018. At the same time, during the actual meeting, the Chilean Church received the pastoral letter from Pope Francis to the pilgrim people of God in Chile. This letter had a strong influence on the local congregations; its language and the considerations contained in it have been the orientation for pastoral work, as has its call to live in a time of spiritual discernment.

Afterward, the Chilean bishops met in July 2018 for their 116th extraordinary general assembly. Against this backdrop, they were invited to initiate a national process of discernment for a more prophetic, synodal, and hope-filled Church. The objective as stated in the document from the Pastoral Commission of the Conference of Chilean Bishops (*Documento de Sistematización*) reads,

> To go on a journey, embark on a process, so that, starting from the deep roots of this crisis and the changes in today's society, we may seek the workings and the will of God for each one of us, our communities, the local Churches and the universal Church on its pilgrimage in Chile, in the awareness of being anointed with the Spirit as the People of God.

The process invited them to create spaces for listening and communal dialogue in the various dioceses, at the level of either diocesan councils, parishes, deaneries, lay movements, or associations. Despite political and social upheavals and the health crisis at national level, parishes throughout the country took part in the project and brought together 5,733 individuals from about 700 communities in Chile.

The methodology used in the process was guided by the verbs proposed by Pope Francis for action: recognize, discern, and choose (*Evangelii Gaudium* 51). Intensive work was done in three overarching areas: "Interpersonal Relationships," "Structure and Management," and "Signs of the Times." Didactic methods in the form of parlor games were suggested for each of these areas and given regional idioms as titles. This created a suitable atmosphere not only for the discussion of complex issues, but also for open and respectful dialogue. It demonstrated that synodal processes can also be experienced through learning by doing.

In 2020 and 2021, the Latin American Assembly of Churches added its newly created listening phase to the national process. Its objective was "to revitalize the Church in a new way through suggestions for change and renewal." However, as this phase coincided with the consultation phases of the diocesan processes, it was difficult to promote it.

Furthermore, the Corona pandemic was an obstacle to cross-regional participation, as many committed pastoral workers had no Internet access or were unable to meet in person, so that the conclusions could not be posted to the feedback website that was the basis for evaluating each phase.

Accordingly, many of the Chilean dioceses tried hard to facilitate participation. Some of them favored copying local bodies of the individual dioceses into the responses sent to the Latin American Assembly of Churches. This was the case in Santiago de Chile, where the discernment process launched in 2020 is linked to the Latin American one and receives contributions from the various consultation formats.

SYNERGISTIC EFFECTS MADE POSSIBLE BY NETWORKING ONGOING PROCESSES

In order to encourage the broadest possible participation, the National Discernment Process will be linked with the diocesan phase of the bishops' synod in Rome "For a Synodal Church: Community, Participation and Mission." This means that the diocesan reports sent to Rome will also serve as input for the Third Church Assembly of Bishops in Chile and their own discernment process. Three documents that complement each other stand out against this backdrop and draw together the processes developed in recent years. One is the "Report on Systematization," which lists the results of national discernment from 2019 and is the most important at national level; the second is the "Twelve Pastoral Challenges" proposed by the Assembly for Latin America and the Caribbean; and finally, the "Synthesis Report" from the Archdiocese of Santiago, the country's most populous diocese.

This report contains the ten topics with which the diocesan assemblies comprising laypeople, priests, and bishops worked most intensively in 2020. First on the list of communal items is the focus on returning to the source of faith: Jesus Christ, who is at the very center of the life for the devout. A further intersecting area is abuse: safeguarding and a procedure for reporting abuse is needed, and also care and compensation for the victims.

As a complement to this, reference is made to the subject of women, central to which is the appreciation of women, which is to be strengthened by their taking on of leadership roles that are acknowledged as such. Connected with this is the triad of power, clericalism, and the position of the laity. The identification of and control over the misuse of power represents an important task, bringing their baptism with the Spirit back to the forefront of renewed awareness for all who received it.

Another focus has young people in view. The appreciation of young people living their faith in a new way is to be acknowledged. They are to be taken seriously as protagonists of evangelization. And not least, poverty and social commitment play an important part in the context of synodal processes. There is a need to provide the necessary funds for those in need. In addition, sharing in the construction of a just society and participation in public debate must be assured. There is a long way to go until these items are implemented, but the course is set.

PRESENCE OF WOMEN IN CHURCH AND SOCIETY

Lebanon

Mirna Abboud Mzawak

For the first time, the Bureau de la Pastorale de la Femme (Pastoral Bureau for Women) in the Patriarchal Curia of the Maronite Church in Lebanon organized a synod on the presence of women in Church and society, thus marking a new focus in the Church, which was already synodal in character beforehand. This has set in motion a process of maturation supported by the patriarch and his staff. Above all, it is an appeal for women to be active participants in Church and society as they seek to put their vocation into practice.

THE GUIDING THREAD running through our synodal process is women as "active faithful." I say this on the basis of my own experience as a witness and protagonist in this synodal process, which has led, for its part, to the official initiation of the Maronite Church Synod. Synodal work, communal reflection, sharing ideas, and the implementation of collective thinking and shared, binding decisions for all has been a constituent element of the Church since its foundation, so it can be said that our Church lives synodally. The Maronite Patriarchal Synod (2005–2006) marks an important stage in the history and life of our Church, which has experienced many synods already. Probably the most famous one is the Lebanese Synod of 1736 (Maronite Patriarchal Synod. Texts and Recommendations, 2006, 7), at which a resolution was passed to the effect that schooling for both girls and boys should be guaranteed on an equal footing.

WHAT WOULD LEBANON BE WITHOUT WOMEN FOR PEACE?

Pope John Paul II, in his postsynodal apostolic exhortation "A New Hope for Lebanon," emphasized that Lebanese women deserve special attention, "to acknowledge their dignity and their rights in the various instances of social and national life" (May 10, 1997, no. 50). He went on to say that women had worn themselves out, above all during the war years, "to protect lives and uphold hopes of peace." Their vocation consisted especially in "being educators for peace."

In this way, women of all religions and denominations had stood up on the front lines for keeping the peace, and supported people in need and refugees. They were proactive in "revolutionary" movements against corruption and in carrying out measures to provide assistance following the tragic explosion in the Port of Beirut on August 4, 2020.

CONDEMNING INJUSTICE AND UNFAIRNESS TOWARD WOMEN

Pope John Paul II's words resonate even more strongly with women when he writes that they need to be involved even more in the life and decisions of the Church and that they are owed greater responsibility than they have been allowed to adopt hitherto. His hope for Lebanon's women is in the emphatic wording of his demand that they should be given the necessary training for this increased responsibility.

This thought is carried forward in the document from the Maronite Patriarchal Synod. In a chapter on the family, there is a section about the role of women with the heading "A new reality for women," in which the Patriarchal Synod emphasizes women's emancipation, now that they are responding to the requirements of a new lifestyle and the necessity of working beyond the home in other fields like education, social work, culture, business and politics, rather than predominantly within the family and domestic sector as in earlier times.

Even though this development is a positive one for women, it has also led to a weakening of their formative role in the family. The relationship to children and the opportunity to be there for them, to be able to respond to their needs, is greatly restricted (Patriarchal Synod no. 29, 356). The same synod challenges married couples and parents to approach the division of duties more functionally in order to maintain family ties. Furthermore, there must be condemnation of the injustice and unfairness under which many women suffer, either by ignoring their human capabilities or treating them with violence, and this happens at all levels whether in the home or at work (357).

WHAT ARE OUR EXPECTATIONS?

I was tasked as a member of the advisory committee to the Maronite Patriarchal Synod with carrying out a study on the way the documents from this synod are received. The main objectives were to create a basis for planning the options after the synod, to deliver clear and informative facts for later synods about the reality of the Maronite Church in all its various components, and to identify and define to what extent the various stakeholders actually understood the synod documents.

This kind of data capture goes along with the entire process. The issue is always what expectations people have in respect of these texts and how they position themselves with regard to the suggested options for action. The majority of respondents expressed the wish to see the development of instruments for research and strategic planning in the Church institutions, especially those that are seen as the direct frame of reference, to guarantee sensible, structured, and sustainable leadership of the socioreligious life of Maronites in Lebanon and the neighboring countries.

The presence of women, their vocation and mission in the Church does not occupy the place due to it, either in the Patriarchal Synod texts from 2003 to 2006 or in other ecclesiastical reference texts from our Maronite Church.

A look at the numbers reporting the presence of women in the Church is ultimately self-explanatory. The results of a study on the presence of women in Maronite parishes and dioceses in Lebanon show that women make up 54 percent of diocesan bodies, 68 percent of parish bodies; 79 percent of groups that take care of children, adolescents, and the elderly; and 73 percent of movements, fraternities, and apostolic associations. By contrast, the presence of women in diocesan or parish administration and governance structures is at a very low level and even declining; women account for only 8 percent in diocesan councils and 25 percent in parish administrative councils.

After a year of very intense reflection work, Bishop Peter Karam, who is responsible for the subject in the Maronite Patriarchal Curia, and members of the Pastoral Bureau for Women, inspired and guided by the Holy Spirit, drew up a kind of roadmap for the implementation of a synodal process on the presence of women in Church and society and presented it to the Maronite Patriarchs.

The Maronite Synod of Bishops, which met in June 2021, then resolved in an official communique to commission the Pastoral Bureau for Women with the organization of a special synodal assembly about women (*Proche Orient*

Chretien, no. 71, 2021). The Synod on Women, Their Presence and Mission in Church and Society officially commenced its work at the generalate of the Maronite Patriarchate in Bkerke in the presence of Patriarch Bechara Boutros al-Rahi, Bishop Peter Karam, other Maronite bishops, and the apostolic nuncio in Lebanon, Archbishop Joseph Spiteri.

HOW CAN WE BRING OUR COOPERATION TO FRUITION?

The main purpose of the Women's Synod is to reflect on the reality of women in our Church and society today. We ask questions about women's motivation for putting their Christian vocation into practice. We are also putting efforts into encouraging active commitment by women to the Church and society, promoting their independence, and reinforcing training to prepare them for their role in administration, positions of leadership, in education, liturgy, and pastoral services. It is also about interpreting the Church's teachings on the subject of women and reaching a deeper understanding of them. And finally, we deliberate on the consolidation of partnership and complementarity in decision-making within the Church.

Various groups have been established in pursuance of these purposes to carry out the Synod's work. As well as strategic support through analyses by different teams of experts, there are research groups in the fields of sociology, anthropology, philosophy, anthropology of religion, practical theology, and statistics. They do field research exercises to accompany the synodal process without reducing it to a research or campaign project.

The synodal core group, made up of members of the Office for Pastoral Care of Women, takes care of the processes in the dioceses and institutions, training, prayer and

Mass texts, and templates for past and future projects and pilots.

ENRICHED BY THE CONGREGATIONS IN COUNTRIES ALONG THE PERSIAN GULF

The Pastoral Committees for Women in the Maronite dioceses in Lebanon that have been established over the years constitute the pillars of synodal work by the structured dissemination of the content of these synods in the parishes. Added to them are the groups of delegates of Maronite communities in the catchment area of the Patriarchate and in the countries of distribution. The parish congregations in the countries along the Persian Gulf that have subscribed to our synodal process are an ecumenical enrichment, as their special feature is their composition from all the patriarchal and Latin Churches of the Middle East.

In addition, several groups of delegates from different institutions have already formed or are currently building up, such as Catholic congregations of women religious, men's congregations, delegates from groups of Catholic schools in Lebanon, Christian associations and apostolic movements, and delegates from NGOs that work with women affected by violence or marginalized in society (*Proche Orient Chretien*, no. 71, 2021).

The synod for, about, and by women, their presence and mission in Church and society represents an important momentum for our Church. It is part of the synodal process for the universal Church. We experience the Maronite Church's women's synod as a gift of grace, in spite of the ongoing suffering and misery of the unprecedented, multistratified crises that Lebanon is going through as never before in modern history.

MEASURING UP TO REALITIES AND PRESERVING UNITY

Senegal

Martin Boucar Tine

The interactions to date in the dioceses of Senegal have shown that Christians share worries and concerns that are very similar to those of their Muslim sisters and brothers. Questions about the proper approach to homosexuality or marginalized social groups, however, are presented in the light of the gospel and the doctrine of the Church. Spirituality is at the core of all synodal efforts in Senegal.

THE CATHOLIC CHURCH in Senegal comprises seven dioceses: Dakar, Thies, Saint-Louis, Tambacounda, Ziguinchor, Kolda, and the Kaolack diocese, where I have served as bishop since November 2018. Only around 10 percent of the population of the country is Christian. But the fact that we constitute a minority does not keep us from fulfilling our vocation of proclaiming the good news to our Senegalese brothers and sisters. We bishops strive to fulfill this mission in a spirit of humility and in synodal coexistence with the faithful for the benefit of a living communion, all the more so now that the pope has called upon us to do so.

On the positive side, we have certainly attained a certain maturity in our faith that transcends the status of a missionary country, as the diocesan synods of Dakar, Ziguinchor, and Kolda as well as the diocesan conferences in the diocese of Kaolack have shown. Yet issues remain that we need to consider in greater detail in future. These include financial responsibility, the training of laypersons with regard to their identity and role in the Church, the situation of women, and questions about society and work as well as on the family, youth, and ecology. The shared struggle around topics that shape the lives of all of us can help us walk our path together in faith, charity, and hope.

For nearly twenty years, our dioceses have worked on the basis of Pastoral Action Plans that chart the course of diocesan life for three, four or even five years. The purpose of these Pastoral Action Plans is to use listening, discernment, training, and commitment to help energize the life of the individual dioceses, in keeping with the intended trilogy of communion, participation, and commitment. This means that the current synodal process in our Churches exhibits a dynamic similar to that of other Churches, each of which follows a path that is specific to them.

The motto for the synodal process of the diocese of Kaolack is built around the process of the Universal Church and reads, “Personal and communal conversion for a synodal Church in communion, participation and mission.” Spirituality is an essential part of our synodal efforts. To us, praying and celebrating together are a way of expressing the notion of “walking together.” Listening to the Holy Spirit, praying to him, and being inspired by him is the spirituality that accompanies the various stages of the synodal process: the opening Mass, the appointment and training of the synodal preparation team (which consists of priests, members of the religious orders, and laypeople), consultation of the parishioners, and merging the results of the diocesan and national phases of interaction.

OWN REALITIES

As the past weeks and months have shown, the pastors in our parishes work closely together and are in close contact with the parishioners. Collaboration is already quite effective in many areas, but it should be further strengthened in the interest of aspects such as participation, solidarity, fraternity, and charity. Since the Church of Christ is one and universal, we consider it necessary to promote not just local and national but also international exchange. This can offer immense enrichment for all involved while supporting the Church of Christ's efforts in "walking together."

Thanks to technology and digitalization, our modern world has become a global village. Still, it is important to acknowledge that every Church, even if it forms part of and exists in solidarity with the Universal Church, has a reality of its own as a result of its own particular historical and local situation. This is a reality that no other reality, no matter how noble or important, can or may obscure. Put quite simply, matters that are of concern to the faithful in the diocese of Kaolack do not necessarily have the same significance elsewhere, and vice versa.

But the exchanges we have had so far have shown us that certain concerns are recurring. They are often the result of misunderstandings and show that we are not always on the same path together. There is concern, on the one hand, for the elderly who can no longer take care of themselves, and on the other for children and young people with few prospects for the future.

One question that causes a great stir among the Senegalese public involves the proper approach to homosexuality. On the one hand, there are attempts to officially recognize the status of homosexual people; on the other hand, there are occasionally violent reactions from those who strictly reject homosexuality and want to banish it from society. The Christian tendency can fluctuate between the two positions without misjudging the Church's position on this question.

Another topic of concern to believers in Senegal is the question of how to approach certain social groups from a Christian point of view. Senegalese society is home to a variety of marginalized groups that have difficulties earning a living because of their unclear social status. These include widows, maids, and servants, for example. Slavery no longer exists in Senegal, but there is a prevalent mentality that prevents people whose ancestors were slaves from assuming certain positions or roles of responsibility. The situation is similar for people who earn their money as linen weavers, shoemakers, artists, or as so-called magicians.

Even more precarious is the situation of people with physical or mental disabilities, or of people who suffer from infectious diseases such as leprosy. Society also has little to no tolerance for drug addicts and (former) prisoners. There is also a kind of social index of people who should be avoided or even eliminated, such as people who are found guilty of theft or are suspected of being witches. Many in Senegal are convinced that if a person suffers from a mysterious illness or experiences misfortune in their career or in love, there must be ghosts or witches involved. Even a Christian would not intervene if faced with a conflict between a person recognized by society and someone from a marginalized group.

Unfortunately, a kind of subliminal racism is widespread even among Christians as well. Senegal may be known as the "land of Teranga" (land of hospitality), but there is widespread distrust of foreigners, or of Senegalese who are not members of one's own ethnic group.

The challenges that society as a whole must confront are reflected in similar ways in the context of the Church. Believers say that women and young people in particular are not listened to attentively enough, and that the needs of the laity are sometimes disregarded. There are also admonitions that the morality of Church officials seems questionable at times. Although consecrated persons are generally trusted and respected, criticisms are sometimes heard that their actions sometimes fall short of those of a "good shepherd" and cast a shadow over their position.

Other topics raised by the believers involve apostasy (renunciation of belief) and the levirate, the custom that obliges a man to marry his deceased brother's widow.

WE ARE ALL MEMBERS OF THE ONE BODY

These few elements derive from a synthesis of replies from our diocese and represent a small cross-section of the things that concern us. It is not difficult to identify themes among them that we share with local Churches on other continents, even if these are not always identical in substance. For example, there is the question of women, to whose views we should devote a more thorough hearing, and of morality at the level of Church officials, a criticism not necessarily always associated with pedophilia.

On the question of specific reforms, how the synodal process will develop remains to be seen. We are still involved in gathering information about our worries and concerns and in conducting a dialogue with all of the people of God. Our aim is to discern what approach the Holy Spirit suggests to us toward the different realities involved. Certainly, the path we take with the Universal Church can also help us find answers to this or that concern, taking our own local ecclesial context into account.

Clearly, we cannot declare ourselves an island within this ecclesiastical structure. We are, and will always remain, interested in the realities and concerns of the others with whom we "walk together," and I would even suggest that in a way they affect us too as fellow members of the one Body of Christ, the Church. Their centuries-old experience can make a great contribution toward making us a Church that attains its full maturity in all its dimensions: in communion, participation, and mission.

A SACRED SPACE FOR MANY, DESPITE CONTROVERSIES

Kenya

Constansia Mumma-Martinon

The Kenyan bishops are following the pope's call and practicing synodality. It has already become clear that the Catholic Church is confronted not just with challenges specific to the African context. Believers are moved by topics such as the role of women or the sexual abuse of minors, just as they are in other parts of the Universal Church. In contrast to Germany, Australia, or Ireland, however, the Church still enjoys a high reputation.

WHEN POPE FRANCIS opened the worldwide Synod on Synodality in Rome on October 9, 2021, the Catholic Church set out on a journey of interaction, reflection, and listening on the African continent as well. Bishop Wilybard Lagho, bishop of the diocese of Malindi, captured Kenya's view of the synodal process: "In the words of Pope Francis, the Synod offers us the opportunity to recognize and listen to our fellow pilgrims. This includes people who believe and pray differently, including as non-Catholics and atheists."

The archdiocese of Nairobi offers a good example of the precise contours of the synodal process in Kenya. Last autumn, Bishop David Kamau appointed a diocesan synodal team to conduct the process; team members include both Church officials and laypeople. From October to April, a variety of activities were held in the different parishes: introduction, data collection, and preparation of a final report for presentation to the deanery and then to the archdiocese. The methodology was focused on the grassroots level. Both individuals and groups of people inside and outside the Church were and are invited to a sharing of views. During the study and the collection of data, care was taken to ensure that the reports would authentically reflect the feelings and concerns of the people.

A synodal team was assembled at Our Lady of Guadalupe Parish in early January; I am in charge of its secretariat. In an effort to reach and inform all of the interested parties involved, we decided to open up a dialogue with the people, working in small groups to discuss the synodal process. Their background situations were quite heterogeneous: there were Catholic and Protestant Christians, believers both with and without prior knowledge; believers who were members of small Christian communities and those who were isolated in their Church. There were Catholics who had been Catholics since birth, Catholics who had joined the Catholic Church in different ways, for example through marriage, and members of other religions.

For those who could not read or write, we translated the questions into Kiswahili and other tribal languages. To facilitate interreligious dialogue, we have regularly invited leaders of other religious communities to dialogue in our Church.

The worldwide synodal path is still in its infancy, but we can already see the firstfruits of dialogue in our parishes. Groups that once had no points of contact are now in contact with each other, and Church members from the outlying districts are becoming more systematically involved. The level of commitment to charity has increased; particularly during Lent, many believers dedicated themselves to strengthening communion among themselves and with people outside the Church. Children and adolescents also became involved in the synodal process in a special way.

A LARGE VARIETY OF TOPICS

As the exchange to date has shown, the spectrum of issues that affect the faithful, and thus the Catholic Church in Kenya, is quite complex. On the one hand, some of the challenges may seem alien to European context. These include polygamy, tribal rivalries, and corruption—factors that divide and paralyze the Church. One example is the 2007 presidential elections, which triggered devastating political unrest in which the Churches took sides and did not sufficiently distance themselves from the political elites.

Along with the cultural challenges we face, the Catholic Church in Kenya also must deal with issues that occur in other parts of the Universal Church as well. This includes the question of the role of women—a particularly troublesome issue, given the traditional and cultural ideologies involved. To this day, Kenyan society expects women to stay at home, look after their children and households, and behave courteously toward their husbands at all times. Education is certainly not a matter of course, and this is why women rarely hold positions of leadership.

This circumstance is reflected in the ecclesial context. Here, too, women are the driving forces of everyday pastoral life. They are in charge of small Christian communities, preside over the parish council, work as catechists to promote the religious education of children, perform charitable service for the poor, and help shape Mass by serving as acolytes and readers. Women evangelize, organize seminars, generate income, collect donations, and sing in Church choirs. They are an indispensable part of the continuation of ecclesial life, yet there is a lack of appreciation for the services they perform, and a lack of consideration of their specific needs.

There is an urgent need to strengthen the role of women, from both a social and a spiritual point of view. Unlike other Churches, such as the Anglican denominations in which women have already been ordained as deacons, unfortunately

Catholic circles have largely avoided addressing the ordination of women, which is absurd given the importance of the issue.

A SEXUAL DOUBLE STANDARD

Just as urgent as the debate around the role of women is the debate about the future character of the lives of priests. For a variety of reasons, celibacy is currently being put to the test. Thus, fewer are answering the call to the priesthood, in some places increasing the size of Churches as the numbers of priests diminishes. There have also been cases in which Catholic priests have become "apostates" after founding Churches of their own in which they do not have to practice celibacy.

Another topic with which young people in particular are constantly struggle is the Church's stance on sexual morality—although it must be pointed out that Kenyan society is still very conservative compared to Europe (particularly where homosexuality is concerned). And whenever the official stances of the Catholic Church and the state diverge, it triggers uncertainty. State-run programs for family planning, for example, that aim to provide everyone—unmarried and young people included—with access to contraception, are vehemently criticized by the Church. As the Church and the government serve the same population, it is essential to rethink Church doctrine on contraception in light of government policy.

That state and ecclesiastical attitudes sometimes stand in contradiction to one another is down to the fact that the Church and the state in Kenya exist separately from one another. The constitution stipulates that there shall be no state religion, and it prohibits religious discrimination. The constitution provides for the right to freedom of religion and worldview for individuals and communities while prohibiting the government from granting preferential status to one religion over another.

Where the point of departure for the Synodal Path in Germany is concerned—the sexual abuse of minors by Church officials—regrettably, it must be noted that this also plays a role in Kenya. The scale is becoming increasingly clear as more and more children, boys in particular, come out and openly discuss what has happened to them. The sad reality is that the accused priests are often simply transferred away and their sexual crimes left unreported to the police.

Recently, during a two-day symposium held at Tangaza University College in Nairobi, the scholar of canon law Father Charles Oloo K'Ochiel stated, "Many cases of child sexual abuse go unreported, with those living in highly rural areas being affected most. Despite the established policies and norms that protect minors, there still remain challenges when it comes to implementation, either due to culture of secrecy that inhibits disclosure, or to a poor monitoring and evaluation framework."

The question of providing more effective protections for children must be addressed in detail, particularly for children whose parents lack the resources required to support their children. An important factor in this connection is certainly the approach taken to power in the ecclesiastical context. By and large, the distribution of power in the Kenyan Church is classically clerical in nature.

The hierarchical structures are firmly fixed and create an impression that there is no room for change. Authority and guidelines come from above, and parishioners have hardly any say at all. It is true that some believers are beginning to question the teachings, authority and power of the Church in various ways. But as the majority is still very conservative, little attention is paid to ideas that run counter to official Church doctrine.

AND YET THE RELATIONSHIP BETWEEN BISHOPS AND THE LAITY IS GOOD

Despite the various controversies, Christians still take a positive attitude toward the Church and the bishops. The majority of bishops seek closeness with the laity, responding to Pope Francis's call to make the Church more synodal. In the eyes of many, the Church is a holy place of hope in which God listens to people's needs and gives them spiritual nourishment. It is also regarded as an important institution for the assistance of people in need.

Awareness of being part of the One, Catholic Universal Church, is very important to believers in Kenya. If the worldwide synodal process is to make the Church truly more synodal and to bear fruit, we must continually remind ourselves of the Christian responsibility we hold in common: we are all called upon to set out on a journey to realize and continue the work of Jesus Christ here on earth. Together, we are the one catholic and apostolic Church. With this in mind, in a poem on the worldwide synodal path, a child from our parish writes,

> This is not an African journey.
> This is not an American journey.
> This is not a European journey.
> This is not an Australian journey.
> This is not an Asian journey.
> But it is a universal journey.
> This is a call to action by local parishes.
> This is called the World Church:
> To travel and pray together,
> We, the Catholic Church, the Universal Church,
> Whose members and children are called upon to
> set out on this path together.

SEARCHING FOR THE HOLY SPIRIT

Australia

John Warhurst

The recommendations of the sexual abuse inquiries are on the table, their implementation is still uncertain. Yet, there is hope that the response of the Australian faithful will be heard. It remains to be seen whether the Australian bishops, despite their different attitudes, will have the courage to initiate reforms.

THE FIFTH PLENARY COUNCIL of the Catholic Church in Australia has just concluded. It began in 2018 with a four-year process in mind but was delayed for a year because of the impact of the COVID-19 pandemic and has since proceeded through several stages of consultation and discernment. A First Assembly of Plenary Council members was held for six days in early October 2021. Because of the pandemic it was not face-to-face, but a hybrid mixture of smaller meetings of members in dioceses and a national online meeting. It concluded with the Second Assembly in Sydney in early July 2022.

DISPIRITED CHURCH

The idea of a Plenary Council had been discussed within the Australian Catholic Bishops Conference (ACBC) for a decade before the decision was taken. Initially it was driven by the decline of the Church in Australia, which a variety of aspects had made increasingly apparent: decline in Mass attendance, falling vocations to the priesthood and religious life, dissatisfaction over the role of women and the involvement of youth. International Church developments also played a role, including the papacy of Pope Francis.

This was compounded by growing calls by the laity for change. In this connection, in recent years, a lay network, the Australian Coalition for Church Reform, gained in significance. As the largest collection of reform-oriented groups, it developed into a platform that gave laypersons a voice and has since garnered the attention of the highest levels of the Church hierarchy.

But the strongest impact on bishops' decision-making came through the state investigation of sexual abuse (Royal Commission into Institutional Responses to Child Sexual Abuse, 2013–2017), which had the Catholic Church as its main focus. The Royal Commission report uncovered extensive child sexual abuse in Catholic institutions and cover-up of these crimes by Church authorities, including bishops.

The report shook up an already dispirited Catholic community and distrust of episcopal authority grew even further. Yet the community of faithful responded energetically to the call by the bishops to take part in a nationwide process of exchange, with a total of 17,500 submissions calling attention to various issues. Some wanted to reinforce the status quo orthodoxy, but the majority mood was for internal and external reform.

THE BISHOPS' ATTITUDES ARE VERY HETEROGENEOUS

Priority issues included internal issues such as governance reform, equality for women in ministry and governance, reform of seminary training and greater adult formation, recognition of the Indigenous Catholic tradition, and liturgical reform. External issues included promotion of integral ecology, solid public leadership, social service, and education, reaching out to minorities and those excluded by the Church, such as divorced and remarried Catholics and the LGBTQ community. The Royal Commission report gave specific advice to the Catholic Church, calling for cultural and structural reform to remedy its child sexual abuse failings and to improve Church leadership and accountability. In turn the Church pledged to respond seriously to the report. The ACBC and Catholic Religious Australia (the peak body for leaders of religious institutes and orders) responded by setting up an international team of advisors to investigate the leadership structures of the Catholic Church of Australia.

In May 2020, the team published its two-hundred-page report: "The Light from the Southern Cross: Promoting Co-responsible Governance in the Catholic Church in Australia," offering a blueprint for widespread reform of governance in dioceses and parishes, built on an examination of synodal theory and practice.

In nearly one hundred detailed recommendations, it addresses modern civic principles of good governance, including coresponsible leadership, consultation with and inclusion of laypersons, financial transparency, and open government. The report also recommends the greater involvement of the people of God in leadership selection, including at the episcopal and parish level, seminary formation, and pastoral planning.

The report was originally meant to be a resource for the Plenary Council but receded into the background and was not integrated directly into the Plenary Council process. It is generally agreed that the agenda of the first Plenary Assembly represented an attempt to address a broad spectrum of topics, but that it did not sufficiently capture the fire and the passion for reforms that had been seen in the contributions of the community of faithful.

The whole Plenary Council process has accentuated tensions between an inner circle and the wider Catholic community over whether the Plenary Council should be an open or closed process.

Control over the process rested with the Bishops' Conference, even though is itself was advised by an executive committee of laypeople, members of religious orders and clergy; practical organization of the Plenary Council was provided by a team headed by a lay representative. The bishops determined the composition and structure of the Council; every step on the path to the First Plenary Assembly was taken only after the Bishops' Conference had granted their approval.

Despite widespread suspicion of the Church hierarchy on the part of reform-oriented laypeople, it is unwise to generalize about the bishops in Australia. They themselves are divided, at times quite clearly, along philosophical and cultural lines that would be familiar to Catholics anywhere, including the United States of America.

The president of the Australian Bishops' Conference, Archbishop Mark Coleridge of Brisbane, has been a strong supporter of a synodal process and an open agenda for the Plenary Council; and Archbishop Tim Costelloe of Perth, a Salesian and president of the Plenary Council, is a much quieter figure. Together, they are attempting to keep the Bishops' Council and the Plenary Council on the same page.

IN MANY RESPECTS A PATCHWORK CHURCH

At one end of a continuum there is a small but powerful group of conservative bishops, of whom the most senior is Archbishop Anthony Fisher of Sydney, vice president of the Australian Bishops' Conference.

At the other end there is one outspokenly progressive bishop, Vincent Long van Nguyen, OFM. Conv. and Bishop of Parramatta (see HK, October 2021, 27–30). The other thirty bishops hold a variety of positions between the two ends of the continuum.

At the diocesan level, the relationship between laity and bishops is variable. There are only a small number of synodal diocesan structures and diocesan pastoral councils. Some bishops, including senior ones, rebuff any attempts to engage with laypersons seeking to challenge orthodox authority and reform old ways of doing things within the Church. Others, including Archbishop Christopher Prowse of Canberra-Goulburn, engage earnestly and constructively. The same diversity holds at the parish level in terms of the relationships between laity and priests and in terms of parish councils.

This variety can be better understood if the character of the Church in Australia is quickly sketched. The Church continues to play a large part in Australian life because about 25 percent of Australians call themselves Catholics, although this number is declining. More than one-fifth of the population of Australia are educated in Catholic schools.

Historically nuns and brothers have provided that schooling and other services to the Catholic community. For many Catholics, schools are the main connection with the Church, more important even than parishes. These religious institutes are a major part of the Australian Church and their often-contentious relationships with bishops an integral part of the Church history of Australia.

The Church is multiethnic, but the Vatican II generation is predominantly Anglo-Celtic, often with an Irish background. The decline in priestly vocations now means that about 50 percent of priests are foreign born, including many from Africa and India. Recently the Church community has been invigorated by immigration, especially from the Indian subcontinent, the Philippines, and Vietnam. The predominantly Latin Rite Church also operates alongside a growing number of Eastern Rite Churches, especially the Maronite Church. This means the Church is increasingly culturally diverse.

The entire Plenary Council was a spiritual event. The core effort involved a search for inspiration by the Holy Spirit based on the question, "What does God expect of us at this time?"

All of the issues were presented in a theological and biblical framework. The guiding methodology of the assemblies has been Ignatian spirituality, with small-group work within the Plenary Council structured around the three stages of spiritual discernment. The emphasis has been on deep listening at all times. Sometimes the emphasis on deep listening has discouraged necessarily robust discussion of issues.

GATHERING ACCORDING TO ROMAN CRITERIA

The Plenary Council itself operated under Vatican rules spelled out in canon law. The 280 members were a mix of bishops, priests, religious, and laypeople. Women and the laity were in the minority, making the Council unrepresentative in a democratic sense, although an increase in lay numbers was possible following consultations with the Vatican.

The proceedings of the Plenary Council were synodal, but according to canon law, only bishops had a deliberative vote. All other votes were consultative only. The impact of this rule was not tested at the First Assembly as the voting was procedural only. At the Second Plenary Assembly, the impacts became quite apparent when the bishops rejected a key portion of the agenda on the role of women in the Church. This rejection was subsequently lifted after the members insisted on another vote and the bishops complied with this.

The rules of procedure led to a discussion at the highest level. This led the Plenary Council Secretary, David Ranson, to ask whether the Australian Church would have been better served by the greater flexibility of a Synod rather than the rigid rules of a Plenary Council. Shortly after the First Assembly of this Plenary Council concluded in October 2021, Pope Francis opened the worldwide synodal path; this put the Church in Australia in an unusual position. The Australian Bishops' Conference advised Catholics to integrate the questions that had arisen in the course of the national exchange phase into the consultation on the Bishops' Synod for the Universal Church.

CONSULTATION FATIGUE AND PROGRESS

For many of the faithful, however, enthusiasm over participation in the worldwide process fell far short of what it had been in the run-up to the Plenary Council as a kind of "consultation fatigue" began to take hold. Others, on the other hand, made their submissions directly to the Synod Secretariat in Rome as they doubted the resonance of their voices within the local process.

Regardless of the strength of participation in the process, the World Synod of Bishops encourages greater awareness of the international dimension of Church renewal.

The Amazonian Synod, the German Synod and other international assemblies are regularly covered in the Australian media, both secular and Church. The same is true of lay initiatives such as the "Root and Branch" lay synod in Bristol.

The hierarchical institutional Church and the lay renewal movement have always had many international connections. The team that composed the report entitled "The Light from the Southern Cross" benefited enormously from its international advisers. The renewal movement Australian Catholic Coalition for Church Reform regularly organizes international talk formats with well-known Catholic speakers, including Mary McAleese, Joan Chittister, and Massimo Faggioli. Even the Australian Ambassador to the Vatican has facilitated an international Zoom conference on Synodality and Women in the Church.

Many questions about genuine synodality in the Church were posed, sometimes painfully, during the Second Plenary Assembly. The outcomes were mixed but generally positive in relation to gender equality and questions of governance and sacramental and liturgical reform, as well as new commitments to recognition of Indigenous spirituality and integral ecology. Expectations within the Catholic community vary, but there is general acknowledgement that we are moving forward.

THE FUTURE REMAINS UNCERTAIN

New Zealand

Joe Grayland

Clericalism, abuse, secularization—New Zealand's Church has immense challenges to overcome. Although reform is inevitable, a new start seems to be farther away than ever. We shall have to wait and see whether the collapse of conventional structures will move laypeople to demand reforms and lend bishops and clerics the necessary impetus to set them in motion.

THE VERY FACT THAT the worldwide synodal pathway began in October 2021, hence in the New Zealand summer season, created the impression in New Zealand that the process is essentially a Northern Hemisphere event. In addition, the end of COVID-19 restrictions in the same timeframe meant that it was even more difficult than otherwise to enthuse people for the synodal process.

However, as the bishops are very much tuned to Pope Francis, and the relationship between them and the faithful is generally positive, many dioceses are trying hard to organize the synodal process in their parishes. In the diocese of Palmerston North, to which I belong, we have organized several small group meetings and asked the participants to respond to the long questionnaire on the diocese's website.

After the summer season, a second attempt was made in March 2022 to integrate more people into the synodal path with the offer of diocese-wide online meetings, albeit with no great success.

The mood among Catholics of both sexes is mixed—and the purpose of the synodal process is not clear. For whom is it intended? For the people, the clergy, the bishops, or the pope? Many Catholics are skeptical as to whether the process is indeed a means of coping with local problems. Others see in it an opportunity to address defects at local and national levels of ecclesiastical life. Others, in turn, hope for changes that will set the Church back in time to what it was before the Second Vatican Council. Different as the expectations are, everyone agrees that something needs to change fundamentally in New Zealand's Catholic Church. Although the faithful are concerned with the four issues of the synodal path in Germany (power and the division of authority, the future design of priestly life, the role of women, and sexual morality of the Church), our starting situation is different.

URGENT NEED FOR REFORM OF CLERICAL STRUCTURES

The greatest concern of Catholics in Aotearoa New Zealand is the structural collapse of ecclesiastical diocesan and parish situations. In most dioceses, there are no longer Eucharistic Masses every Sunday due to the lack of priests. In addition, the decline in attendance at Mass and the absence of young people results in congregations shrinking and parishes being merged together. One priest has to be in charge of several parishes that can be up to 150 kilometers apart. This situation has led to a stronger involvement of laypeople in the administration of pastoral life. In many places, laypeople lead Sunday liturgical worship and hand out communion.

The dysfunctional structure of the Church restricts its ability to deliver sacramental services to the faithful. The issue of who can be ordained and the rationale of access qualifications for offices requiring ordination are associated with this. Subjects such as obligatory celibacy and the reservation of ordination to men only are obstacles to winning indigenous people for service in their local Churches.

DEVASTATING ABUSE OF POWER IN THE CONTEXT OF CHURCH AND STATE

In consequence, young men from Southeast Asia, especially from Vietnam and India, are brought in to fill the gap in the number of seminarians, which changes the nature of the local Church and of the body of priests. New waves of immigration means the return of a Church with intense piety.

At the end of the day, the subject of problematic clerical structures in Aotearoa New Zealand is the critical driving force behind the synodal process. Basically, it can be said that the latter is driven here, as in Germany, not by the necessity to listen, but by the necessity for reform of the clerical structure. In the wake of any such reform, all the issues connected with clerical status must be thoroughly reconsidered. This includes subjects like marriage, sexuality, recruitment, training, postordination formation, and the integration of nonindigenous priests.

Reform of this kind is urgently required, not only due to the structural collapse of the dioceses. Various forms of abuse of power have unfortunately brought a great deal of harm upon the people. In 2018, the Prime Minister Jacinda Ardern set up a Royal Commission of Inquiry to investigate psychological, physical, and sexual abuse in state institutions. At the request of the Church, the inquiry was extended to include a review of Church institutions.

Two years ago, the Commission's first interim report confirmed the fear that the indigenous population, which counts itself as approximately 800,000 people, is particularly badly affected. According to the report, up to 253,000 people were subjected to abuse between 1958 and 2010, the great majority being children and adolescents, 80 percent of them Māori children. Violence against children—often in association with drug and alcohol abuse—is, sadly, a widespread problem in New Zealand. According to UNICEF, almost one-third of children have no access to hot water and only poor health and nutrition care.

NO REVOLT AMONG PEOPLE OF THE CHURCH DESPITE INDIGNATION

Reacting to the interim report from the government Commission, the Catholic Church commissioned an investigation of its own in 2020 about abuse in Church institutions. The results were published at the beginning of this year. Eighty percent of the 1122 victims were children. Half of them were sexually abused. In total, 14 percent of diocesan priests and 8 percent of all male and 3 percent of all female members of religious orders were accused, whereby most of the reported cases of mistreatment were alleged to have taken place in the sixties and seventies.

As with the collapse of parish structures, the scandal of abuse lies in the dysfunctional clerical structure. Added to this is a mentality according to which the Church deserves special treatment because of its prominent position. As in the state context, systematic cover-ups were the means of choice to get a grip on the issue of child abuse. What this meant in most of the specific cases was that the alleged abuser was transferred with no fear of further consequences.

WILL THEY BE ABLE TO FULLY FACE THEIR DARK SIDE?

The Royal Commission Inquiry is still ongoing. The interim results have not yet raised a wave of movement for fundamental changes within the Church. In contrast to Germany, the United States, and Australia, where court proceedings and a commission of inquiry on the abuse of minors and Church power has driven forward the synodal pathway, this has not happened in Aotearoa New Zealand.

The New Zealand Catholic Church is not a significant voice in the public debate and political life. As a result of the strict separation of Church and state and the secular culture, it is a secondary voice that is mostly viewed as irrelevant by political opinion bearers. Public sympathy with the position of the Catholic Church is generally low and the political will to defend it is minimal.

As far as the future shape of the Church is concerned, we can only hope that Catholics in New Zealand succeed in jumping over their own shadow and stand up for change in view of the structural collapse of parish congregations. Equally, it remains to be seen whether the statement from the archbishop of Wellington, Cardinal John Dew, that he is "deeply ashamed" by the abuse, yet "determined to build up a safe Church for all," will be followed up with action. Let us hope that the Holy Spirit will grant everyone the necessary upwind.

WILL THE SYNODAL PATH HELP US OUT OF THE CRISIS?

Luxembourg

Théo Péporté

Concentrated competency: Germany has drafted a model for a synodal Church that can radiate out to other countries.

THE CZECH SOCIOLOGIST and priest Tomaš Halik puts it in a nutshell when he writes that the great ship of yesterday's Christianity is going down, and warns against wasting time. "If anyone thinks that the present storms surrounding sexual abuse are going to pass and that everything will return to what it was before" they are deceiving themselves (HK, August 2019, 26). Does the Synodal Path represent an opportunity to renew the Church and lead it out of its crisis? Will it be able to have effects outside Germany? The occasion could not be more serious. The revelation of years and years of sexual abuse by Catholic priests, deacons, and religious, and its systemic causes, have shattered those with responsibility and prompted many members to leave the Church. The loss of confidence is immense.

We have long known that every kind of abuse is always abuse of power. That is why it will not be sufficient to speak about power and the division of authority in the Church. A way of controlling power, rethinking and reorganizing the structures of power, has to be found. This is the only way to regain trust. That is why the subject of power and division of authority is, for me, the crucial one, especially as the other topics of the Synodal Path are all connected with it in one way or another: the image of priesthood, the long overdue issue of justice for women in the Church, and questions of relationships and sexuality.

Are these German matters with effects only on the German Church? Certainly not. A glance at the media in other countries is enough to see that the same issues are raised in many countries around the world with varying emphasis and in different cultural and political contexts. So, if the Synodal Path leads to a positive outcome, the Church in Germany will have performed a valuable service to the universal Church.

Sophisticated text templates constitute the basis for the discussions. Texts for orientation, foundation, action—all these formats have in common the fact that they are drafted with the utmost care and precision, displaying their respective topic cleanly on a sound theological basis and pointing out clear options. A great deal of work and sound knowledge goes into them. And even though I understand that some people find them hard and describe them as too complicated, I take the view that arguments need to be voiced at this level. After completion of the Synodal Path, a summary of the results can be drawn up in more accessible language. Yet, it is still worthwhile to read the extant original texts and work through them for oneself.

A further plus is that all the templates can be viewed on the internet in multiple languages at www.synodalerweg.de. This transparent manner of proceeding enables people outside Germany to share in tracking every development and following every line of thought.

After three out of five scheduled Synodal Assemblies, I am impressed and remain optimistic. The arguments are put forward openly, intelligently, and authoritatively, definitely controversially, but nevertheless respectfully. Everyone has their say, and anything can be said. Even the front lines are becoming clearer, the tension between supporters of a traditional, conservative image of the Church and the advocates of renewal is becoming better defined. Up to now, it has been a pretty fair debate except for a small number of skirmishes. The Synodal Assemblies are wrestling with the question as to what is to remain and what is to come. This controversy will gain in intensity as the process goes forward. I can only hope that the culture of debate that has worked relatively well so far will continue to bear fruit, and that attempts from outside to influence it will not undermine the Synodal Path.

Church is more than the Synodal Path, dispute, crisis, and loss of trust. First and foremost, the spiritual impulses and acts of worship during the Synodal Assemblies demonstrate this. They lead everyone together and focus anew on the true Lord of the Church as a whole. That is a good thing.

PATHS OF DIVERSITY

A global Church needs subsidiarity

Frank Ronge

THE CATHOLIC CHURCH is in an existential crisis. This crisis was not spawned by abuse—let alone by the fact that the abuse has been made public. Rather, the abuse and cover-up are what make this crisis manifest. Globally, even if at staggered intervals. The crisis is a crisis of leadership, a structural crisis, a crisis of faith. In many cases there is a discrepancy in the Church, between life and discourse, and between faith and proclamation. This is true of sexual abuse and the approach taken to deal with it; it is also true of sexual morality, the definition of gender roles, the life of celibacy, the way money and power are handled, and many other things. In the eyes of internal observers—and external observers all the more so—the Church appears to have entered a downward spiral that has since led to lethargy or departures on the part of the "core congregation" as well as full-time and voluntary staff. In Germany, this is evidenced by the precise figures on people who have left the Church as recorded here. Many wonder whether the Church truly believes what it preaches. There are massive questions about the legitimacy of actions taken by the Church.

There needs to be a genuine evolution in ecclesial culture, and this evolution must begin with a change in mentality, especially among those in positions of responsibility. There needs to be a culture of dialogue—and spaces in which it can take shape. This culture includes honesty and open-mindedness, a willingness to listen and look closely while at the same time setting defensive reflexes aside—and, above all, truthfulness. The new culture includes the courage to make mistakes, as Pope Francis describes it using the term of the "bruised" Church. This is precisely the aim of the Synodal Path of the Catholic Church in Germany: to practice a new culture. It might still be a little tentative and searching, and there may be setbacks. The Synodal Path seeks to conceptualize the specific Church reforms that are needed here and now, in an effort to bring people the experience of the good news.

The Synodal Path is a path for Germany. It does not purport to offer a master plan for synodality worldwide—even if the same questions are of equal importance in other countries. And its resolutions will also be related to the concrete situation in Germany. Even within the Church, globalization makes us believe that the rapid exchange of information is accompanied by a global capacity to manage it. But real life remains tied to one place. The legitimacy of action by the Church is not just a result of the message's worthiness of acknowledgment; it also requires de facto acknowledgment on the part of the local people. In its social doctrine, the Church emphatically advocates the principle of subsidiarity, which begins by requiring that the things that can be addressed on a smaller scale within a community should indeed be dealt with at that level. Responsibility for this must also remain at this level. This inevitably and deliberately promotes a variety of ways of life. The subsidiarity principle is also fundamental to the communion of the Church. Of course, this right bears upon the independent rules that are in place, not upon the core tenets of faith. As some historical transformations have shown, however, this core must not be defined too broadly, either. The relationship between unity, necessary uniformity and possible variety must be redefined. If the aspect of subsidiarity applies, preventing interventions from on high, then the other aspect that gives the principle its name applies as well: that the higher level must aid with independent rules, assisting directly in the interest of diversity. It is good that the Roman synodal secretariat has announced that it will assist local Churches with the creation of synodality. But what is true of the forms by which synodality is put into practice must also be true of the reforms required at the local level. These reforms must be not merely approved but actively supported.

This book makes diversity visible. The diversity of our livelihood. A Church that sounds out diversity in a synodal manner and grasps universality in a subsidiary manner will be in a position to bear concrete, local witness to the one, unifying hope.

CONTRIBUTORS

Dr. Rafael Luciani is professor at Universidad Católica Andrés Bello in Caracas, Venezuela, and at the Boston College School of Theology and Ministry in Boston, Massachusetts (USA). He is a theological adviser to the Episcopal Council of Latin America (CELAM) and to the Theological Commission of the General Secretariat of the Synod of Bishops.

Sister Dr. Joan Chittister was born in 1936. A Benedictine sister, she entered Erie Monastery in Pennsylvania at the age of sixteen. The author of more than sixty books is considered a courageous, passionate, energetic, and sought-after speaker, commentator, and advisor. For more than forty-five years, the recipient of the Hans Küng Award has been committed to the promotion of peace, equality, and justice for all peoples, across all religions.

Birgit Weiler, Dr. theol., was born in 1958. She is a member of the Medical Mission Sisters and a theologian; she teaches in the Academic Department of Theology at the Pontifical Catholic University of Peru in Lima. As a member of the group of theologians in CELAM, among other things, she was extensively involved in the process of listening to one another, as well as in the First Ecclesial Assembly. She was instrumental in the preparation of the two documents for joint reflection within the context of the Assembly.

Christina Kheng teaches pastoral theology and leadership at the East Asian Pastoral Institute in Manila and assists religious organizations in the areas of leadership, management, and community discernment. She has a PhD in theology from the Australian Catholic University. Her current research focuses on interdisciplinary methodology in Church-society dialogue. She is an advisory member of the Pontifical Commission for Methodology.

Thomas Söding, Dr. theol., was born in 1956 and is professor for New Testament Studies at the University of Bochum. He was a member of the Commissio Theologica Internationalis from 2004 until 2014. He has been vice president of the Central Committee of German Catholics since 2021, by virtue of which he is also a president of the Synodal Path of the Catholic Church in Germany.

Mario Grech, born in 1957, is a canonist and was bishop of Gozo (Malta) from 2005 to 2020. In 2020, Pope Francis appointed him secretary general of the Synod of Bishops and created him a cardinal. Therefore, in Rome he is also responsible for the Synod 2021–2023: "For a Synodal Church: Communion, Participation and Mission."

Dr. Franz-Josef Bode was born in 1951. He has been bishop of Osnabrück since 1995 and vice chairman of the German Bishops' Conference since 2017. In the Synodal Path he is a member of the Synodal Presidency and cochairman of Synodal Forum III, "Women in Ministries and Offices in the Church."

Daniel Kosch, Dr. theol., was born in 1958. He is a theologian and secretary general of the Roman Catholic Central Conference of Switzerland. He is taking part in the Synodal Path as an international observer, at the invitation of the German Bishops' Conference and the Central Committee of German Catholics.

Paule Zellitch (b. 1953) is a theologian and president of the Conférence Catholique des Baptisé.e.s Francophones. She is a cofounder of the Atelier de lecture biblique (Bible-reading workshop) in Paris and teaches at the Institut Catholique de Paris (Catholic University of Paris). She was the first layperson to be elected vice coordinator of the European Vocational Congress (Europäisches Berufungskongress). From 2006 to 2012 she was editor-in-chief of a journal of practical theology published by the Bishops' Conference of France. At the same time, she informally held the position of deputy director of the Service national des vocations (National Vocations Service) and worked as an expert for the Catholic Press Association.

Czesław Kozon was born in 1951 and has been bishop of Copenhagen since 1995. He comes from a family with Polish roots. He studied theology at Pontifical Gregorian University and Pontifical Lateran University from 1971 through 1977. He is currently president of the Nordic Bishops' Conference. As an observer of the German Synodal Path, he regularly attends the Synodal Assemblies in Frankfurt.

Dr. Luis Manuel Romero Sánchez was born in 1974. He earned a doctoral degree in biblical theology from the Pontifical Gregorian University in Rome. Since 2017, he has been director of the Secretariat of the Episcopal Commission for Laypersons, Family, and Life of the Spanish Bishops' Conference (CEE) and advisor to the Spanish Laity Forum. He served as coordinator of the national Congress of the Laity in 2020, a capacity in which he was largely responsible for organizational matters. He is secretary of the Synodal Team of the CEE, which is coordinating work for the next Synod of Bishops.

Mauro Castagnaro was born in 1963 and works as an educator and sociologist at Il cuore di Crema, an organization for the rehabilitation of drug addicts. A political scientist and journalist by training, he is committed to pacifism, international solidarity, and ecumenism. His journalistic work has specialized in the economic, social, political, and ecclesial situation in Latin America. He regularly publishes numerous writings by commission of the Italian section of the We Are Church movement, of which he is the deputy national coordinator.

Katarína Hulmanová, Msc. (Eng), is a trained computer programmer and theologian. Alongside bringing up five children she has been president of the Forum of Christian Institutions, Secretary of the European Laity Forum, and a member of the Pontifical Council for the Laity. She has played a significant role in creating the Pastoral Plan of the Church in Slovakia. She currently works on a voluntary basis as secretary of the Social Subcommittee of the Theological Commission of the Bishops' Conference of Slovakia. She is also involved in assisting needy people and raising young people‘s awareness of poverty.

Nicola Brady, born 1980, is chair of the Steering Committee for the Irish National Synodal Assembly. She was appointed general secretary of the umbrella organization Churches Together in Britain and Ireland. Brady is director of Christian Aid Ireland and the Maximilian-Kolbe-Stiftung, which works to apply the lessons of post–World War II German-Polish reconciliation to other areas of conflict.

Rene Reid was born in 1944, studied theology, is a former religious sister and cofoundress and director of the Catholic Church Reform International network. She taught Catholic religious instruction for many years, established a successful network marketing organization, and was one of the first female talk show hosts in the United States of America. She advocates support for people to find their own meaning in life and, as an elected official, is a key person in providing for the homeless in her community. Reid represents the whole strategy team of Catholic Church Reform International, whose members shared in preparing this article.

Msgr. Didier Berthet was born in 1962 and has been bishop of Saint-Dié since 2016.

Jérôme Vignon was born in 1944. From 2007 to 2016 he served as president, and is now honorary president, of the French Lay Movement, Semaines sociales de France.

Carolina Bacher Martínez, born in 1966, she has a doctoral degree in pastoral theology and teaches as a professor in the Faculty of Theology at the Universidad Católica Argentina. She is a member of the scientific committee of the Teologanda program, and also vice president of the Argentine Theological Society (2019–2022).

Catalina Cerda-Planas has an MA in theology and political science. She is currently reading for a doctoral degree at the Pontificia Universidad Católica in Chile and the Julius Maximilian University of Würzburg. She is a scientific assistant at the Institut für Weltkirche und Mission in Sankt Georgen, Frankfurt and the Universidad Católica Silva Henriquez in Santiago de Chile.

Pascale Larré has an MA in theology and philosophy. She teaches at the Pontificia Universidad Católica in Chile. She is currently the national executive secretary for the youth and vocations division of the Chilean Province of the Jesuits.

Mirna Abboud Mzawak teaches and does research at the Holy Spirit University of Kaslik (USEK), where she is head of the Department of Psychology and Social Science in the Faculty of Art and (Natural) Science. She is the coordinator of the Pastoral Bureau for Women in the Patriarchal Curia of the Maronite Church in Bkerke and a member of the Maronite Patriarchal Synod Committee. She is also a member of the Maronite Research and Documentation Center (CMDR). She holds a doctorate in social science and works in several research projects in the fields of youth, women, sustainable development, urban administration, families, and culture.

Bishop Martin Boucar Tine was born in Senegal in 1968 and ordained to the priesthood in 1996. He is a member of the Congregation of the Blessed Sacrament and has been bishop of the diocese of Kaolack since 2018. He taught dogmatics for eight years in Kinshasa before living in Rome for many years, where he served as general councilor of the Congregation of the Blessed Sacrament. His special area of commitment is interreligious dialogue.

Dr. Constansia Mumma-Martinon (b. 1967) teaches political science and public administration at the University of Nairobi. She holds a doctorate in political science from Leipzig University and received a postgraduate diploma in diplomacy and international relations in Nairobi. She has taught at a variety of universities including the European University for Peace in Austria. She is assisting with the execution of the synodal process in the diocese of Nairobi and is in charge of the synodal secretariat of her home parish.

John Warhurst (b. 1948) is an Emeritus Professor of Political Science at the Australian National University and a Plenary Council Member. He has written two books on Church renewal in Australia and the Plenary Council. In 2017, in response to the study on sexual abuse, he founded the reform movement Concerned Catholics Canberra Goulburn, part of a large lay network, and Australasian Catholic Coalition for Church Reform, which for several decades has dedicated its efforts to renewal of the Church along the lines of the Second Vatican Council.

Joe Grayland (b. 1963) is a priest in the Palmerston North diocese in New Zealand and took his doctoral degree in Münster in liturgical science in 1997. Grayland is the author of several books and articles. He operates the channel "Flashes of Insight," giving information on current developments worldwide in the Catholic Church.

Théo Péporté (b. 1953) is the former press spokesman and head of the Communications and Press Office of the Catholic Church in

Luxembourg is an observer of the Synodal Path. He worked previously in adult education and as a media advisor. He is a member of the Council of Bishops in the Archdiocese of Luxembourg.

Frank Ronge was born in 1968 and has been head of the Doctrine and Education Section of the German Bishops' Conference since 2010. A theologian and political scientist, he has been in charge of the Office of the Synodal Path of the German Bishops' Conference since its inception and the Central Committee of German Catholics.